The Tragedie of
King Lear

By Edward de Vere

Art:
Portrait of Edward de Vere
17th Earl of Oxford (1550-1604)

This edition produced by
Verus Publishing

V | P

www.verusbooks.com

ISBN: 978-1-951267-40-7
Imprint / Publisher: Verus Publishing

The Author

Edward de Vere, 17th Earl of Oxford

Beiography and Bibliography
After the Play

A Preverse

Drone on ye learned scholars of the day
As to with whom the words ahead the credit lay.
For our part though can be no further doubt
That the author of these words has been found out
To be a person lordly and refined
On whom the light of wit so boldly shined
That to keep this wit from tearing in the fray
He gave another, lesser wit his say.

Now let the least of wits
That writes these paltry lines
Yield to him whose peerless name
Should be with reverence spake.
Let this name be not of history's misassigns
Whose pen and verse have made the earth to shake.

The Tragedie of
King Lear

By Edward de Vere

The Main Characters

King Lear - The King of Britain

The Earl of Gloucester

The Earl of Kent - Also disguised as Caius

Fool - Lear's fool

Edgar - Son of Gloucester

Edmund - Illegitimate son of Gloucester

Goneril - Lear's eldest daughter

Regan - Lear's second daughter

Cordelia - Lear's youngest daughter

Duke of Albany - Goneril's husband

Duke of Cornwall - Regan's husband

Gentleman - Attendant to Cordelia

Oswald - Steward of Goneril

King of France - Suitor to Cordelia

Duke of Burgundy - Suitor to Cordelia

Old man - Tenant of Gloucester

Curan - A Courtier

And now, the Play...

ACT I

SCENE I.

King Lear's palace.

Enter KENT, GLOUCESTER, and EDMUND

KENT

I thought the king had more affected the Duke of
Albany than Cornwall.

GLOUCESTER

It did always seem so to us: but now, in the
division of the kingdom, it appears not which of
the dukes he values most; for equalities are so
weighed, that curiosity in neither can make choice
of either's moiety.

KENT

Is not this your son, my lord?

GLOUCESTER

His breeding, sir, hath been at my charge: I have
so often blushed to acknowledge him, that now I am
brazed to it.

KENT

I cannot conceive you.

GLOUCESTER

Sir, this young fellow's mother could: whereupon
she grew round-wombed, and had, indeed, sir, a son
for her cradle ere she had a husband for her bed.
Do you smell a fault?

KENT

I cannot wish the fault undone, the issue of it
being so proper.

GLOUCESTER

But I have, sir, a son by order of law, some year

elder than this, who yet is no dearer in my account: though this knave came something saucily into the world before he was sent for, yet was his mother fair; there was good sport at his making, and the whoreson must be acknowledged. Do you know this noble gentleman, Edmund?

EDMUND

No, my lord.

GLOUCESTER

My lord of Kent: remember him hereafter as my honourable friend.

EDMUND

My services to your lordship.

KENT

I must love you, and sue to know you better.

EDMUND

Sir, I shall study deserving.

GLOUCESTER

He hath been out nine years, and away he shall again. The king is coming.

Sennet. Enter KING LEAR, CORNWALL, ALBANY, GONERIL, REGAN, CORDELIA, and Attendants

KING LEAR

Attend the lords of France and Burgundy, Gloucester.

GLOUCESTER

I shall, my liege.

Exeunt GLOUCESTER and EDMUND

KING LEAR

Meantime we shall express our darker purpose.
Give me the map there. Know that we have divided
In three our kingdom: and 'tis our fast intent

To shake all cares and business from our age;
Conferring them on younger strengths, while we
Unburthen'd crawl toward death. Our son of Cornwall,
And you, our no less loving son of Albany,
We have this hour a constant will to publish
Our daughters' several dowers, that future strife
May be prevented now. The princes, France and
Burgundy,
Great rivals in our youngest daughter's love,
Long in our court have made their amorous sojourn,
And here are to be answer'd. Tell me, my daughters,--
Since now we will divest us both of rule,
Interest of territory, cares of state,--
Which of you shall we say doth love us most?
That we our largest bounty may extend
Where nature doth with merit challenge. Goneril,
Our eldest-born, speak first.
GONERIL
Sir, I love you more than words can wield the matter;
Dearer than eye-sight, space, and liberty;
Beyond what can be valued, rich or rare;
No less than life, with grace, health, beauty, honour;
As much as child e'er loved, or father found;
A love that makes breath poor, and speech unable;
Beyond all manner of so much I love you.
CORDELIA
[Aside] What shall Cordelia do?
Love, and be silent.
KING LEAR
Of all these bounds, even from this line to this,
With shadowy forests and with champains rich'd,
With plenteous rivers and wide-skirted meads,
We make thee lady: to thine and Albany's issue
Be this perpetual. What says our second daughter,

Our dearest Regan, wife to Cornwall? Speak.

REGAN

Sir, I am made
Of the self-same metal that my sister is,
And prize me at her worth. In my true heart
I find she names my very deed of love;
Only she comes too short: that I profess
Myself an enemy to all other joys,
Which the most precious square of sense possesses;
And find I am alone felicitate
In your dear highness' love.

CORDELIA

[Aside]   Then poor Cordelia!
And yet not so; since, I am sure, my love's
More richer than my tongue.

KING LEAR

To thee and thine hereditary ever
Remain this ample third of our fair kingdom;
No less in space, validity, and pleasure,
Than that conferr'd on Goneril. Now, our joy,
Although the last, not least; to whose young love
The vines of France and milk of Burgundy
Strive to be interess'd; what can you say to draw
A third more opulent than your sisters? Speak.

CORDELIA

Nothing, my lord.

KING LEAR

Nothing!

CORDELIA

Nothing.

KING LEAR

Nothing will come of nothing: speak again.

CORDELIA

Unhappy that I am, I cannot heave

My heart into my mouth: I love your majesty
According to my bond; nor more nor less.
KING LEAR
How, how, Cordelia! mend your speech a little,
Lest it may mar your fortunes.
CORDELIA
Good my lord,
You have begot me, bred me, loved me: I
Return those duties back as are right fit,
Obey you, love you, and most honour you.
Why have my sisters husbands, if they say
They love you all? Haply, when I shall wed,
That lord whose hand must take my plight shall carry
Half my love with him, half my care and duty:
Sure, I shall never marry like my sisters,
To love my father all.
KING LEAR
But goes thy heart with this?
CORDELIA
Ay, good my lord.
KING LEAR
So young, and so untender?
CORDELIA
So young, my lord, and true.
KING LEAR
Let it be so; thy truth, then, be thy dower:
For, by the sacred radiance of the sun,
The mysteries of Hecate, and the night;
By all the operation of the orbs
From whom we do exist, and cease to be;
Here I disclaim all my paternal care,
Propinquity and property of blood,
And as a stranger to my heart and me
Hold thee, from this, for ever. The barbarous Scythian,

Or he that makes his generation messes
To gorge his appetite, shall to my bosom
Be as well neighbour'd, pitied, and relieved,
As thou my sometime daughter.

KENT

Good my liege,--

KING LEAR

Peace, Kent!
Come not between the dragon and his wrath.
I loved her most, and thought to set my rest
On her kind nursery. Hence, and avoid my sight!
So be my grave my peace, as here I give
Her father's heart from her! Call France; who stirs?
Call Burgundy. Cornwall and Albany,
With my two daughters' dowers digest this third:
Let pride, which she calls plainness, marry her.
I do invest you jointly with my power,
Pre-eminence, and all the large effects
That troop with majesty. Ourself, by monthly course,
With reservation of an hundred knights,
By you to be sustain'd, shall our abode
Make with you by due turns. Only we still retain
The name, and all the additions to a king;
The sway, revenue, execution of the rest,
Beloved sons, be yours: which to confirm,
This coronet part betwixt you.

Giving the crown

KENT

Royal Lear,
Whom I have ever honour'd as my king,
Loved as my father, as my master follow'd,
As my great patron thought on in my prayers,--

KING LEAR

The bow is bent and drawn, make from the shaft.

KENT

Let it fall rather, though the fork invade
The region of my heart: be Kent unmannerly,
When Lear is mad. What wilt thou do, old man?
Think'st thou that duty shall have dread to speak,
When power to flattery bows? To plainness honour's bound,
When majesty stoops to folly. Reverse thy doom;
And, in thy best consideration, cheque
This hideous rashness: answer my life my judgment,
Thy youngest daughter does not love thee least;
Nor are those empty-hearted whose low sound
Reverbs no hollowness.

KING LEAR

Kent, on thy life, no more.

KENT

My life I never held but as a pawn
To wage against thy enemies; nor fear to lose it,
Thy safety being the motive.

KING LEAR

Out of my sight!

KENT

See better, Lear; and let me still remain
The true blank of thine eye.

KING LEAR

Now, by Apollo,--

KENT

Now, by Apollo, king,
Thou swear'st thy gods in vain.

KING LEAR

O, vassal! miscreant!

Laying his hand on his sword

ALBANY and CORNWALL

    Dear sir, forbear.

KENT

    Do:

    Kill thy physician, and the fee bestow

    Upon thy foul disease. Revoke thy doom;

    Or, whilst I can vent clamour from my throat,

    I'll tell thee thou dost evil.

KING LEAR

    Hear me, recreant!

    On thine allegiance, hear me!

    Since thou hast sought to make us break our vow,

    Which we durst never yet, and with strain'd pride

    To come between our sentence and our power,

    Which nor our nature nor our place can bear,

    Our potency made good, take thy reward.

    Five days we do allot thee, for provision

    To shield thee from diseases of the world;

    And on the sixth to turn thy hated back

    Upon our kingdom: if, on the tenth day following,

    Thy banish'd trunk be found in our dominions,

    The moment is thy death. Away! by Jupiter,

    This shall not be revoked.

KENT

    Fare thee well, king: sith thus thou wilt appear,

    Freedom lives hence, and banishment is here.

To CORDELIA

The gods to their dear shelter take thee, maid,

That justly think'st, and hast most rightly said!

To REGAN and GONERIL

And your large speeches may your deeds approve,

13

That good effects may spring from words of love.
Thus Kent, O princes, bids you all adieu;
He'll shape his old course in a country new.

Exit

*Flourish. Re-enter GLOUCESTER, with KING OF
FRANCE, BURGUNDY, and Attendants*

GLOUCESTER
Here's France and Burgundy, my noble lord.
KING LEAR
My lord of Burgundy.
We first address towards you, who with this king
Hath rivall'd for our daughter: what, in the least,
Will you require in present dower with her,
Or cease your quest of love?
BURGUNDY
Most royal majesty,
I crave no more than what your highness offer'd,
Nor will you tender less.
KING LEAR
Right noble Burgundy,
When she was dear to us, we did hold her so;
But now her price is fall'n. Sir, there she stands:
If aught within that little seeming substance,
Or all of it, with our displeasure pieced,
And nothing more, may fitly like your grace,
She's there, and she is yours.
BURGUNDY
I know no answer.
KING LEAR
Will you, with those infirmities she owes,
Unfriended, new-adopted to our hate,

Dower'd with our curse, and stranger'd with our oath,
Take her, or leave her?
BURGUNDY
Pardon me, royal sir;
Election makes not up on such conditions.
KING LEAR
Then leave her, sir; for, by the power that made me,
I tell you all her wealth.

To KING OF FRANCE

For you, great king,
I would not from your love make such a stray,
To match you where I hate; therefore beseech you
To avert your liking a more worthier way
Than on a wretch whom nature is ashamed
Almost to acknowledge hers.
KING OF FRANCE
This is most strange,
That she, that even but now was your best object,
The argument of your praise, balm of your age,
Most best, most dearest, should in this trice of time
Commit a thing so monstrous, to dismantle
So many folds of favour. Sure, her offence
Must be of such unnatural degree,
That monsters it, or your fore-vouch'd affection
Fall'n into taint: which to believe of her,
Must be a faith that reason without miracle
Could never plant in me.
CORDELIA
I yet beseech your majesty,--
If for I want that glib and oily art,
To speak and purpose not; since what I well intend,
I'll do't before I speak,--that you make known
It is no vicious blot, murder, or foulness,

15

No unchaste action, or dishonour'd step,
That hath deprived me of your grace and favour;
But even for want of that for which I am richer,
A still-soliciting eye, and such a tongue
As I am glad I have not, though not to have it
Hath lost me in your liking.

KING LEAR
Better thou
Hadst not been born than not to have pleased me better.

KING OF FRANCE
Is it but this,--a tardiness in nature
Which often leaves the history unspoke
That it intends to do? My lord of Burgundy,
What say you to the lady? Love's not love
When it is mingled with regards that stand
Aloof from the entire point. Will you have her?
She is herself a dowry.

BURGUNDY
Royal Lear,
Give but that portion which yourself proposed,
And here I take Cordelia by the hand,
Duchess of Burgundy.

KING LEAR
Nothing: I have sworn; I am firm.

BURGUNDY
I am sorry, then, you have so lost a father
That you must lose a husband.

CORDELIA
Peace be with Burgundy!
Since that respects of fortune are his love,
I shall not be his wife.

KING OF FRANCE
Fairest Cordelia, that art most rich, being poor;
Most choice, forsaken; and most loved, despised!

Thee and thy virtues here I seize upon:
Be it lawful I take up what's cast away.
Gods, gods! 'tis strange that from their cold'st neglect
My love should kindle to inflamed respect.
Thy dowerless daughter, king, thrown to my chance,
Is queen of us, of ours, and our fair France:
Not all the dukes of waterish Burgundy
Can buy this unprized precious maid of me.
Bid them farewell, Cordelia, though unkind:
Thou losest here, a better where to find.

KING LEAR

Thou hast her, France: let her be thine; for we
Have no such daughter, nor shall ever see
That face of hers again. Therefore be gone
Without our grace, our love, our benison.
Come, noble Burgundy.

Flourish. Exeunt all but KING OF FRANCE, GONERIL,
REGAN, and CORDELIA

KING OF FRANCE

Bid farewell to your sisters.

CORDELIA

The jewels of our father, with wash'd eyes
Cordelia leaves you: I know you what you are;
And like a sister am most loath to call
Your faults as they are named. Use well our father:
To your professed bosoms I commit him
But yet, alas, stood I within his grace,
I would prefer him to a better place.
So, farewell to you both.

REGAN

Prescribe not us our duties.

GONERIL

Let your study

17

Be to content your lord, who hath received you
At fortune's alms. You have obedience scanted,
And well are worth the want that you have wanted.
CORDELIA
Time shall unfold what plaited cunning hides:
Who cover faults, at last shame them derides.
Well may you prosper!
KING OF FRANCE
Come, my fair Cordelia.

Exeunt KING OF FRANCE and CORDELIA

GONERIL
Sister, it is not a little I have to say of what
most nearly appertains to us both. I think our
father will hence to-night.
REGAN
That's most certain, and with you; next month with us.
GONERIL
You see how full of changes his age is; the
observation we have made of it hath not been
little: he always loved our sister most; and
with what poor judgment he hath now cast her off
appears too grossly.
REGAN
'Tis the infirmity of his age: yet he hath ever
but slenderly known himself.
GONERIL
The best and soundest of his time hath been but
rash; then must we look to receive from his age,
not alone the imperfections of long-engraffed
condition, but therewithal the unruly waywardness
that infirm and choleric years bring with them.
REGAN
Such unconstant starts are we like to have from

him as this of Kent's banishment.

GONERIL

There is further compliment of leavetaking
between France and him. Pray you, let's hit
together: if our father carry authority with
such dispositions as he bears, this last
surrender of his will but offend us.

REGAN

We shall further think on't.

GONERIL

We must do something, and i' the heat.

Exeunt

SCENE II.

The Earl of Gloucester's castle.

Enter EDMUND, with a letter

EDMUND

Thou, nature, art my goddess; to thy law
My services are bound. Wherefore should I
Stand in the plague of custom, and permit
The curiosity of nations to deprive me,
For that I am some twelve or fourteen moon-shines
Lag of a brother? Why bastard? wherefore base?
When my dimensions are as well compact,
My mind as generous, and my shape as true,
As honest madam's issue? Why brand they us
With base? with baseness? bastardy? base, base?
Who, in the lusty stealth of nature, take
More composition and fierce quality
Than doth, within a dull, stale, tired bed,
Go to the creating a whole tribe of fops,
Got 'tween asleep and wake? Well, then,

19

Legitimate Edgar, I must have your land:
Our father's love is to the bastard Edmund
As to the legitimate: fine word,--legitimate!
Well, my legitimate, if this letter speed,
And my invention thrive, Edmund the base
Shall top the legitimate. I grow; I prosper:
Now, gods, stand up for bastards!

Enter GLOUCESTER

GLOUCESTER
Kent banish'd thus! and France in choler parted!
And the king gone to-night! subscribed his power!
Confined to exhibition! All this done
Upon the gad! Edmund, how now! what news?
EDMUND
So please your lordship, none.

Putting up the letter

GLOUCESTER
Why so earnestly seek you to put up that letter?
EDMUND
I know no news, my lord.
GLOUCESTER
What paper were you reading?
EDMUND
Nothing, my lord.
GLOUCESTER
No? What needed, then, that terrible dispatch of
it into your pocket? the quality of nothing hath
not such need to hide itself. Let's see: come,
if it be nothing, I shall not need spectacles.
EDMUND
I beseech you, sir, pardon me: it is a letter

from my brother, that I have not all o'er-read;
and for so much as I have perused, I find it not
fit for your o'er-looking.

GLOUCESTER

Give me the letter, sir.

EDMUND

I shall offend, either to detain or give it. The
contents, as in part I understand them, are to blame.

GLOUCESTER

Let's see, let's see.

EDMUND

I hope, for my brother's justification, he wrote
this but as an essay or taste of my virtue.

GLOUCESTER

[Reads] 'This policy and reverence of age makes
the world bitter to the best of our times; keeps
our fortunes from us till our oldness cannot relish
them. I begin to find an idle and fond bondage
in the oppression of aged tyranny; who sways, not
as it hath power, but as it is suffered. Come to
me, that of this I may speak more. If our father
would sleep till I waked him, you should half his
revenue for ever, and live the beloved of your
brother,   Edgar.'
Hum--conspiracy!--'Sleep till I waked him,--you
should enjoy half his revenue,'--My son Edgar!
Had he a hand to write this? a heart and brain
to breed it in?--When came this to you? who
brought it?

EDMUND

It was not brought me, my lord; there's the
cunning of it; I found it thrown in at the
casement of my closet.

GLOUCESTER

You know the character to be your brother's?

EDMUND

If the matter were good, my lord, I durst swear
it were his; but, in respect of that, I would
fain think it were not.

GLOUCESTER

It is his.

EDMUND

It is his hand, my lord; but I hope his heart is
not in the contents.

GLOUCESTER

Hath he never heretofore sounded you in this business?

EDMUND

Never, my lord: but I have heard him oft
maintain it to be fit, that, sons at perfect age,
and fathers declining, the father should be as
ward to the son, and the son manage his revenue.

GLOUCESTER

O villain, villain! His very opinion in the
letter! Abhorred villain! Unnatural, detested,
brutish villain! worse than brutish! Go, sirrah,
seek him; I'll apprehend him: abominable villain!
Where is he?

EDMUND

I do not well know, my lord. If it shall please
you to suspend your indignation against my
brother till you can derive from him better
testimony of his intent, you shall run a certain
course; where, if you violently proceed against
him, mistaking his purpose, it would make a great
gap in your own honour, and shake in pieces the
heart of his obedience. I dare pawn down my life
for him, that he hath wrote this to feel my
affection to your honour, and to no further

pretence of danger.

GLOUCESTER

Think you so?

EDMUND

If your honour judge it meet, I will place you
where you shall hear us confer of this, and by an
auricular assurance have your satisfaction; and
that without any further delay than this very evening.

GLOUCESTER

He cannot be such a monster--

EDMUND

Nor is not, sure.

GLOUCESTER

To his father, that so tenderly and entirely
loves him. Heaven and earth! Edmund, seek him
out: wind me into him, I pray you: frame the
business after your own wisdom. I would unstate
myself, to be in a due resolution.

EDMUND

I will seek him, sir, presently: convey the
business as I shall find means and acquaint you withal.

GLOUCESTER

These late eclipses in the sun and moon portend
no good to us: though the wisdom of nature can
reason it thus and thus, yet nature finds itself
scourged by the sequent effects: love cools,
friendship falls off, brothers divide: in
cities, mutinies; in countries, discord; in
palaces, treason; and the bond cracked 'twixt son
and father. This villain of mine comes under the
prediction; there's son against father: the king
falls from bias of nature; there's father against
child. We have seen the best of our time:
machinations, hollowness, treachery, and all

ruinous disorders, follow us disquietly to our
graves. Find out this villain, Edmund; it shall
lose thee nothing; do it carefully. And the
noble and true-hearted Kent banished! his
offence, honesty! 'Tis strange.

Exit

EDMUND
This is the excellent foppery of the world, that,
when we are sick in fortune,--often the surfeit
of our own behavior,--we make guilty of our
disasters the sun, the moon, and the stars: as
if we were villains by necessity; fools by
heavenly compulsion; knaves, thieves, and
treachers, by spherical predominance; drunkards,
liars, and adulterers, by an enforced obedience of
planetary influence; and all that we are evil in,
by a divine thrusting on: an admirable evasion
of whoremaster man, to lay his goatish
disposition to the charge of a star! My
father compounded with my mother under the
dragon's tail; and my nativity was under Ursa
major; so that it follows, I am rough and
lecherous. Tut, I should have been that I am,
had the maidenliest star in the firmament
twinkled on my bastardizing. Edgar--

Enter EDGAR

And pat he comes like the catastrophe of the old
comedy: my cue is villanous melancholy, with a
sigh like Tom o' Bedlam. O, these eclipses do
portend these divisions! fa, sol, la, mi.
EDGAR

How now, brother Edmund! what serious
contemplation are you in?
EDMUND

I am thinking, brother, of a prediction I read
this other day, what should follow these eclipses.
EDGAR

Do you busy yourself about that?
EDMUND

I promise you, the effects he writes of succeed
unhappily; as of unnaturalness between the child
and the parent; death, dearth, dissolutions of
ancient amities; divisions in state, menaces and
maledictions against king and nobles; needless
diffidences, banishment of friends, dissipation
of cohorts, nuptial breaches, and I know not what.
EDGAR

How long have you been a sectary astronomical?
EDMUND

Come, come; when saw you my father last?
EDGAR

Why, the night gone by.
EDMUND

Spake you with him?
EDGAR

Ay, two hours together.
EDMUND

Parted you in good terms? Found you no
displeasure in him by word or countenance?
EDGAR

None at all.
EDMUND

Bethink yourself wherein you may have offended
him: and at my entreaty forbear his presence
till some little time hath qualified the heat of

his displeasure; which at this instant so rageth
in him, that with the mischief of your person it
would scarcely allay.

EDGAR

Some villain hath done me wrong.

EDMUND

That's my fear. I pray you, have a continent
forbearance till the spied of his rage goes
slower; and, as I say, retire with me to my
lodging, from whence I will fitly bring you to
hear my lord speak: pray ye, go; there's my key:
if you do stir abroad, go armed.

EDGAR

Armed, brother!

EDMUND

Brother, I advise you to the best; go armed: I
am no honest man if there be any good meaning
towards you: I have told you what I have seen
and heard; but faintly, nothing like the image
and horror of it: pray you, away.

EDGAR

Shall I hear from you anon?

EDMUND

I do serve you in this business.

Exit EDGAR

A credulous father! and a brother noble,
Whose nature is so far from doing harms,
That he suspects none: on whose foolish honesty
My practises ride easy! I see the business.
Let me, if not by birth, have lands by wit:
All with me's meet that I can fashion fit.

Exit

SCENE III.

The Duke of Albany's palace.

Enter GONERIL, and OSWALD, her steward

GONERIL

Did my father strike my gentleman for chiding of his
fool?

OSWALD

Yes, madam.

GONERIL

By day and night he wrongs me; every hour
He flashes into one gross crime or other,
That sets us all at odds: I'll not endure it:
His knights grow riotous, and himself upbraids us
On every trifle. When he returns from hunting,
I will not speak with him; say I am sick:
If you come slack of former services,
You shall do well; the fault of it I'll answer.

OSWALD

He's coming, madam; I hear him.

Horns within

GONERIL

Put on what weary negligence you please,
You and your fellows; I'll have it come to question:
If he dislike it, let him to our sister,
Whose mind and mine, I know, in that are one,
Not to be over-ruled. Idle old man,
That still would manage those authorities
That he hath given away! Now, by my life,
Old fools are babes again; and must be used
With cheques as flatteries,--when they are seen abused.
Remember what I tell you.

OSWALD

Well, madam.

GONERIL

And let his knights have colder looks among you;
What grows of it, no matter; advise your fellows so:
I would breed from hence occasions, and I shall,
That I may speak: I'll write straight to my sister,
To hold my very course. Prepare for dinner.

Exeunt

SCENE IV.

A hall in the same.

Enter KENT, disguised

KENT

If but as well I other accents borrow,
That can my speech defuse, my good intent
May carry through itself to that full issue
For which I razed my likeness. Now, banish'd Kent,
If thou canst serve where thou dost stand condemn'd,
So may it come, thy master, whom thou lovest,
Shall find thee full of labours.

Horns within. Enter KING LEAR, Knights, and Attendants

KING LEAR

Let me not stay a jot for dinner; go get it ready.

Exit an Attendant

How now! what art thou?

KENT

A man, sir.

KING LEAR

What dost thou profess? what wouldst thou with us?

KENT

    I do profess to be no less than I seem; to serve
    him truly that will put me in trust: to love him
    that is honest; to converse with him that is wise,
    and says little; to fear judgment; to fight when I
    cannot choose; and to eat no fish.

KING LEAR

    What art thou?

KENT

    A very honest-hearted fellow, and as poor as the king.

KING LEAR

    If thou be as poor for a subject as he is for a
    king, thou art poor enough. What wouldst thou?

KENT

    Service.

KING LEAR

    Who wouldst thou serve?

KENT

    You.

KING LEAR

    Dost thou know me, fellow?

KENT

    No, sir; but you have that in your countenance
    which I would fain call master.

KING LEAR

    What's that?

KENT

    Authority.

KING LEAR

    What services canst thou do?

KENT

    I can keep honest counsel, ride, run, mar a curious
    tale in telling it, and deliver a plain message
    bluntly: that which ordinary men are fit for, I am

qualified in; and the best of me is diligence.

KING LEAR

How old art thou?

KENT

Not so young, sir, to love a woman for singing, nor
so old to dote on her for any thing: I have years
on my back forty eight.

KING LEAR

Follow me; thou shalt serve me: if I like thee no
worse after dinner, I will not part from thee yet.
Dinner, ho, dinner! Where's my knave? my fool?
Go you, and call my fool hither.

Exit an Attendant

Enter OSWALD

You, you, sirrah, where's my daughter?

OSWALD

So please you,--

Exit

KING LEAR

What says the fellow there? Call the clotpoll back.

Exit a Knight

Where's my fool, ho? I think the world's asleep.

Re-enter Knight

How now! where's that mongrel?

Knight

He says, my lord, your daughter is not well.

KING LEAR

Why came not the slave back to me when I called him.

Knight

Sir, he answered me in the roundest manner, he would
not.

KING LEAR

He would not!

Knight

My lord, I know not what the matter is; but, to my
judgment, your highness is not entertained with that
ceremonious affection as you were wont; there's a
great abatement of kindness appears as well in the
general dependants as in the duke himself also and
your daughter.

KING LEAR

Ha! sayest thou so?

Knight

I beseech you, pardon me, my lord, if I be mistaken;
for my duty cannot be silent when I think your
highness wronged.

KING LEAR

Thou but rememberest me of mine own conception: I
have perceived a most faint neglect of late; which I
have rather blamed as mine own jealous curiosity
than as a very pretence and purpose of unkindness:
I will look further into't. But where's my fool? I
have not seen him this two days.

Knight

Since my young lady's going into France, sir, the
fool hath much pined away.

KING LEAR

No more of that; I have noted it well. Go you, and
tell my daughter I would speak with her.
Exit an Attendant

Go you, call hither my fool.

Exit an Attendant

Re-enter OSWALD

O, you sir, you, come you hither, sir: who am I,
sir?
KING LEAR

OSWALD

My lady's father.
KING LEAR

'My lady's father'! my lord's knave: your
whoreson dog! you slave! you cur!
OSWALD

I am none of these, my lord; I beseech your pardon.
KING LEAR

Do you bandy looks with me, you rascal?

Striking him

OSWALD

I'll not be struck, my lord.
KENT

Nor tripped neither, you base football player.

Tripping up his heels

KING LEAR

I thank thee, fellow; thou servest me, and I'll
love thee.
KENT

Come, sir, arise, away! I'll teach you differences:
away, away! if you will measure your lubber's
length again, tarry: but away! go to; have you
wisdom? so.

Pushes OSWALD out

KING LEAR
Now, my friendly knave, I thank thee: there's
earnest of thy service.

Giving KENT money

Enter Fool

Fool
Let me hire him too: here's my coxcomb.
Offering KENT his cap

KING LEAR
How now, my pretty knave! how dost thou?
Fool
Sirrah, you were best take my coxcomb.
KENT
Why, fool?
Fool
Why, for taking one's part that's out of favour:
nay, an thou canst not smile as the wind sits,
thou'lt catch cold shortly: there, take my coxcomb:
why, this fellow has banished two on's daughters,
and did the third a blessing against his will; if
thou follow him, thou must needs wear my coxcomb.
How now, nuncle! Would I had two coxcombs and two
daughters!
KING LEAR
Why, my boy?
Fool
If I gave them all my living, I'ld keep my coxcombs
myself. There's mine; beg another of thy daughters.

KING LEAR

Take heed, sirrah; the whip.

Fool

Truth's a dog must to kennel; he must be whipped
out, when Lady the brach may stand by the fire and
stink.

KING LEAR

A pestilent gall to me!

Fool

Sirrah, I'll teach thee a speech.

KING LEAR

Do.

Fool

Mark it, nuncle:
Have more than thou showest,
Speak less than thou knowest,
Lend less than thou owest,
Ride more than thou goest,
Learn more than thou trowest,
Set less than thou throwest;
Leave thy drink and thy whore,
And keep in-a-door,
And thou shalt have more
Than two tens to a score.

KENT

This is nothing, fool.

Fool

Then 'tis like the breath of an unfee'd lawyer; you
gave me nothing for't. Can you make no use of
nothing, nuncle?

KING LEAR

Why, no, boy; nothing can be made out of nothing.

Fool

[To KENT] Prithee, tell him, so much the rent of

his land comes to: he will not believe a fool.

KING LEAR

A bitter fool!

Fool

Dost thou know the difference, my boy, between a
bitter fool and a sweet fool?

KING LEAR

No, lad; teach me.

Fool

That lord that counsell'd thee
To give away thy land,
Come place him here by me,
Do thou for him stand:
The sweet and bitter fool
Will presently appear;
The one in motley here,
The other found out there.

KING LEAR

Dost thou call me fool, boy?

Fool

All thy other titles thou hast given away; that
thou wast born with.

KENT

This is not altogether fool, my lord.

Fool

No, faith, lords and great men will not let me; if
I had a monopoly out, they would have part on't:
and ladies too, they will not let me have all fool
to myself; they'll be snatching. Give me an egg,
nuncle, and I'll give thee two crowns.

KING LEAR

What two crowns shall they be?

Fool

Why, after I have cut the egg i' the middle, and eat

up the meat, the two crowns of the egg. When thou
clovest thy crown i' the middle, and gavest away
both parts, thou borest thy ass on thy back o'er
the dirt: thou hadst little wit in thy bald crown,
when thou gavest thy golden one away. If I speak
like myself in this, let him be whipped that first
finds it so.

Singing

Fools had ne'er less wit in a year;
For wise men are grown foppish,
They know not how their wits to wear,
Their manners are so apish.
KING LEAR
When were you wont to be so full of songs, sirrah?
Fool
I have used it, nuncle, ever since thou madest thy
daughters thy mothers: for when thou gavest them
the rod, and put'st down thine own breeches,

Singing

Then they for sudden joy did weep,
And I for sorrow sung,
That such a king should play bo-peep,
And go the fools among.
Prithee, nuncle, keep a schoolmaster that can teach
thy fool to lie: I would fain learn to lie.
KING LEAR
An you lie, sirrah, we'll have you whipped.
Fool
I marvel what kin thou and thy daughters are:
they'll have me whipped for speaking true, thou'lt
have me whipped for lying; and sometimes I am

whipped for holding my peace. I had rather be any
kind o' thing than a fool: and yet I would not be
thee, nuncle; thou hast pared thy wit o' both sides,
and left nothing i' the middle: here comes one o'
the parings.

Enter GONERIL

KING LEAR

How now, daughter! what makes that frontlet on?
Methinks you are too much of late i' the frown.

Fool

Thou wast a pretty fellow when thou hadst no need to
care for her frowning; now thou art an O without a
figure: I am better than thou art now; I am a fool,
thou art nothing.

To GONERIL

Yes, forsooth, I will hold my tongue; so your face
bids me, though you say nothing. Mum, mum,
He that keeps nor crust nor crum,
Weary of all, shall want some.

Pointing to KING LEAR

That's a shealed peascod.

GONERIL

Not only, sir, this your all-licensed fool,
But other of your insolent retinue
Do hourly carp and quarrel; breaking forth
In rank and not-to-be endured riots. Sir,
I had thought, by making this well known unto you,
To have found a safe redress; but now grow fearful,
By what yourself too late have spoke and done.
That you protect this course, and put it on

By your allowance; which if you should, the fault
Would not 'scape censure, nor the redresses sleep,
Which, in the tender of a wholesome weal,
Might in their working do you that offence,
Which else were shame, that then necessity
Will call discreet proceeding.

Fool

For, you trow, nuncle,
The hedge-sparrow fed the cuckoo so long,
That it's had it head bit off by it young.
So, out went the candle, and we were left darkling.

KING LEAR

Are you our daughter?

GONERIL

Come, sir,
I would you would make use of that good wisdom,
Whereof I know you are fraught; and put away
These dispositions, that of late transform you
From what you rightly are.

Fool

May not an ass know when the cart
draws the horse? Whoop, Jug! I love thee.

KING LEAR

Doth any here know me? This is not Lear:
Doth Lear walk thus? speak thus? Where are his eyes?
Either his notion weakens, his discernings
Are lethargied--Ha! waking? 'tis not so.
Who is it that can tell me who I am?

Fool

Lear's shadow.

KING LEAR

I would learn that; for, by the
marks of sovereignty, knowledge, and reason,
I should be false persuaded I had daughters.

Fool

Which they will make an obedient father.

KING LEAR

Your name, fair gentlewoman?

GONERIL

This admiration, sir, is much o' the savour
Of other your new pranks. I do beseech you
To understand my purposes aright:
As you are old and reverend, you should be wise.
Here do you keep a hundred knights and squires;
Men so disorder'd, so debosh'd and bold,
That this our court, infected with their manners,
Shows like a riotous inn: epicurism and lust
Make it more like a tavern or a brothel
Than a graced palace. The shame itself doth speak
For instant remedy: be then desired
By her, that else will take the thing she begs,
A little to disquantity your train;
And the remainder, that shall still depend,
To be such men as may besort your age,
And know themselves and you.

KING LEAR

Darkness and devils!
Saddle my horses; call my train together:
Degenerate bastard! I'll not trouble thee.
Yet have I left a daughter.

GONERIL

You strike my people; and your disorder'd rabble
Make servants of their betters.

Enter ALBANY

KING LEAR

Woe, that too late repents,--

To ALBANY

O, sir, are you come?
Is it your will? Speak, sir. Prepare my horses.
Ingratitude, thou marble-hearted fiend,
More hideous when thou show'st thee in a child
Than the sea-monster!
ALBANY
    Pray, sir, be patient.
KING LEAR
    [To GONERIL] Detested kite! thou liest.
My train are men of choice and rarest parts,
That all particulars of duty know,
And in the most exact regard support
The worships of their name. O most small fault,
How ugly didst thou in Cordelia show!
That, like an engine, wrench'd my frame of nature
From the fix'd place; drew from heart all love,
And added to the gall. O Lear, Lear, Lear!
Beat at this gate, that let thy folly in,

Striking his head

And thy dear judgment out! Go, go, my people.
ALBANY
    My lord, I am guiltless, as I am ignorant
Of what hath moved you.
KING LEAR
    It may be so, my lord.
Hear, nature, hear; dear goddess, hear!
Suspend thy purpose, if thou didst intend
To make this creature fruitful!
Into her womb convey sterility!
Dry up in her the organs of increase;
And from her derogate body never spring

A babe to honour her! If she must teem,
Create her child of spleen; that it may live,
And be a thwart disnatured torment to her!
Let it stamp wrinkles in her brow of youth;
With cadent tears fret channels in her cheeks;
Turn all her mother's pains and benefits
To laughter and contempt; that she may feel
How sharper than a serpent's tooth it is
To have a thankless child! Away, away!

Exit

ALBANY
Now, gods that we adore, whereof comes this?
GONERIL
Never afflict yourself to know the cause;
But let his disposition have that scope
That dotage gives it.

Re-enter KING LEAR

KING LEAR
What, fifty of my followers at a clap!
Within a fortnight!
ALBANY
What's the matter, sir?
KING LEAR
I'll tell thee:

To GONERIL

Life and death! I am ashamed
That thou hast power to shake my manhood thus;
That these hot tears, which break from me perforce,
Should make thee worth them. Blasts and fogs upon
thee!

The untented woundings of a father's curse
Pierce every sense about thee! Old fond eyes,
Beweep this cause again, I'll pluck ye out,
And cast you, with the waters that you lose,
To temper clay. Yea, it is come to this?
Let is be so: yet have I left a daughter,
Who, I am sure, is kind and comfortable:
When she shall hear this of thee, with her nails
She'll flay thy wolvish visage. Thou shalt find
That I'll resume the shape which thou dost think
I have cast off for ever: thou shalt,
I warrant thee.

Exeunt KING LEAR, KENT, and Attendants

GONERIL
    Do you mark that, my lord?
ALBANY
    I cannot be so partial, Goneril,
    To the great love I bear you,--
GONERIL
    Pray you, content. What, Oswald, ho!

To the Fool

    You, sir, more knave than fool, after your master.
Fool
    Nuncle Lear, nuncle Lear, tarry and take the fool
    with thee.
    A fox, when one has caught her,
    And such a daughter,
    Should sure to the slaughter,
    If my cap would buy a halter:
    So the fool follows after.

Exit

42

GONERIL

This man hath had good counsel:--a hundred knights!
'Tis politic and safe to let him keep
At point a hundred knights: yes, that, on every dream,
Each buzz, each fancy, each complaint, dislike,
He may enguard his dotage with their powers,
And hold our lives in mercy. Oswald, I say!

ALBANY

Well, you may fear too far.

GONERIL

Safer than trust too far:
Let me still take away the harms I fear,
Not fear still to be taken: I know his heart.
What he hath utter'd I have writ my sister
If she sustain him and his hundred knights
When I have show'd the unfitness,--

Re-enter OSWALD

How now, Oswald!
What, have you writ that letter to my sister?

OSWALD

Yes, madam.

GONERIL

Take you some company, and away to horse:
Inform her full of my particular fear;
And thereto add such reasons of your own
As may compact it more. Get you gone;
And hasten your return.

Exit OSWALD

No, no, my lord,
This milky gentleness and course of yours

Though I condemn not, yet, under pardon,
You are much more attask'd for want of wisdom
Than praised for harmful mildness.

ALBANY

How far your eyes may pierce I can not tell:
Striving to better, oft we mar what's well.

GONERIL

Nay, then--

ALBANY

Well, well; the event.

Exeunt

SCENE V.

Court before the same.

Enter KING LEAR, KENT, and Fool

KING LEAR

Go you before to Gloucester with these letters.
Acquaint my daughter no further with any thing you
know than comes from her demand out of the letter.
If your diligence be not speedy, I shall be there afore
you.

KENT

I will not sleep, my lord, till I have delivered
your letter.

Exit

Fool

If a man's brains were in's heels, were't not in
danger of kibes?

KING LEAR

Ay, boy.

Fool

Then, I prithee, be merry; thy wit shall ne'er go
slip-shod.

KING LEAR

Ha, ha, ha!

Fool

Shalt see thy other daughter will use thee kindly;
for though she's as like this as a crab's like an
apple, yet I can tell what I can tell.

KING LEAR

Why, what canst thou tell, my boy?

Fool

She will taste as like this as a crab does to a
crab. Thou canst tell why one's nose stands i'
the middle on's face?

KING LEAR

No.

Fool

Why, to keep one's eyes of either side's nose; that
what a man cannot smell out, he may spy into.

KING LEAR

I did her wrong--

Fool

Canst tell how an oyster makes his shell?

KING LEAR

No.

Fool

Nor I neither; but I can tell why a snail has a house.

KING LEAR

Why?

Fool

Why, to put his head in; not to give it away to his
daughters, and leave his horns without a case.

KING LEAR

I will forget my nature. So kind a father! Be my
horses ready?

Fool

Thy asses are gone about 'em. The reason why the
seven stars are no more than seven is a pretty reason.

KING LEAR

Because they are not eight?

Fool

Yes, indeed: thou wouldst make a good fool.

KING LEAR

To take 't again perforce! Monster ingratitude!

Fool

If thou wert my fool, nuncle, I'ld have thee beaten
for being old before thy time.

KING LEAR

How's that?

Fool

Thou shouldst not have been old till thou hadst
been wise.

KING LEAR

O, let me not be mad, not mad, sweet heaven
Keep me in temper: I would not be mad!

Enter Gentleman

How now! are the horses ready?

Gentleman

Ready, my lord.

KING LEAR

Come, boy.

Fool

She that's a maid now, and laughs at my departure,
Shall not be a maid long, unless things be cut shorter.

Exeunt

ACT II

SCENE I.

GLOUCESTER's castle.

Enter EDMUND, and CURAN meets him

EDMUND
Save thee, Curan.

CURAN
And you, sir. I have been with your father, and
given him notice that the Duke of Cornwall and Regan
his duchess will be here with him this night.

EDMUND
How comes that?

CURAN
Nay, I know not. You have heard of the news abroad;
I mean the whispered ones, for they are yet but
ear-kissing arguments?

EDMUND
Not I pray you, what are they?

CURAN
Have you heard of no likely wars toward, 'twixt the
Dukes of Cornwall and Albany?

EDMUND
Not a word.

CURAN
You may do, then, in time. Fare you well, sir.

Exit

EDMUND
The duke be here to-night? The better! best!
This weaves itself perforce into my business.

My father hath set guard to take my brother;
And I have one thing, of a queasy question,
Which I must act: briefness and fortune, work!
Brother, a word; descend: brother, I say!

Enter EDGAR

My father watches: O sir, fly this place;
Intelligence is given where you are hid;
You have now the good advantage of the night:
Have you not spoken 'gainst the Duke of Cornwall?
He's coming hither: now, i' the night, i' the haste,
And Regan with him: have you nothing said
Upon his party 'gainst the Duke of Albany?
Advise yourself.

EDGAR

I am sure on't, not a word.

EDMUND

I hear my father coming: pardon me:
In cunning I must draw my sword upon you
Draw; seem to defend yourself; now quit you well.
Yield: come before my father. Light, ho, here!
Fly, brother. Torches, torches! So, farewell.

Exit EDGAR

Some blood drawn on me would beget opinion.

Wounds his arm

Of my more fierce endeavour: I have seen drunkards
Do more than this in sport. Father, father!
Stop, stop! No help?

Enter GLOUCESTER, and Servants with torches

GLOUCESTER

Now, Edmund, where's the villain?
EDMUND
   Here stood he in the dark, his sharp sword out,
   Mumbling of wicked charms, conjuring the moon
   To stand auspicious mistress,--
GLOUCESTER
   But where is he?
EDMUND
   Look, sir, I bleed.
GLOUCESTER
   Where is the villain, Edmund?
EDMUND
   Fled this way, sir. When by no means he could--
GLOUCESTER
   Pursue him, ho! Go after.

Exeunt some Servants

By no means what?
EDMUND
   Persuade me to the murder of your lordship;
   But that I told him, the revenging gods
   'Gainst parricides did all their thunders bend;
   Spoke, with how manifold and strong a bond
   The child was bound to the father; sir, in fine,
   Seeing how loathly opposite I stood
   To his unnatural purpose, in fell motion,
   With his prepared sword, he charges home
   My unprovided body, lanced mine arm:
   But when he saw my best alarum'd spirits,
   Bold in the quarrel's right, roused to the encounter,
   Or whether gasted by the noise I made,
   Full suddenly he fled.
GLOUCESTER
   Let him fly far:

Not in this land shall he remain uncaught;
And found--dispatch. The noble duke my master,
My worthy arch and patron, comes to-night:
By his authority I will proclaim it,
That he which finds him shall deserve our thanks,
Bringing the murderous coward to the stake;
He that conceals him, death.

EDMUND

When I dissuaded him from his intent,
And found him pight to do it, with curst speech
I threaten'd to discover him: he replied,
'Thou unpossessing bastard! dost thou think,
If I would stand against thee, would the reposal
Of any trust, virtue, or worth in thee
Make thy words faith'd? No: what I should deny,--
As this I would: ay, though thou didst produce
My very character,--I'ld turn it all
To thy suggestion, plot, and damned practise:
And thou must make a dullard of the world,
If they not thought the profits of my death
Were very pregnant and potential spurs
To make thee seek it.'

GLOUCESTER

Strong and fasten'd villain
Would he deny his letter? I never got him.

Tucket within

Hark, the duke's trumpets! I know not why he comes.
All ports I'll bar; the villain shall not 'scape;
The duke must grant me that: besides, his picture
I will send far and near, that all the kingdom
May have the due note of him; and of my land,
Loyal and natural boy, I'll work the means
To make thee capable.

Enter CORNWALL, REGAN, and Attendants

CORNWALL
>How now, my noble friend! since I came hither,
>Which I can call but now, I have heard strange news.

REGAN
>If it be true, all vengeance comes too short
>Which can pursue the offender. How dost, my lord?

GLOUCESTER
>O, madam, my old heart is crack'd, it's crack'd!

REGAN
>What, did my father's godson seek your life?
>He whom my father named? your Edgar?

GLOUCESTER
>O, lady, lady, shame would have it hid!

REGAN
>Was he not companion with the riotous knights
>That tend upon my father?

GLOUCESTER
>I know not, madam: 'tis too bad, too bad.

EDMUND
>Yes, madam, he was of that consort.

REGAN
>No marvel, then, though he were ill affected:
>'Tis they have put him on the old man's death,
>To have the expense and waste of his revenues.
>I have this present evening from my sister
>Been well inform'd of them; and with such cautions,
>That if they come to sojourn at my house,
>I'll not be there.

CORNWALL
>Nor I, assure thee, Regan.
>Edmund, I hear that you have shown your father
>A child-like office.

EDMUND
  'Twas my duty, sir.
GLOUCESTER
  He did bewray his practise; and received
  This hurt you see, striving to apprehend him.
CORNWALL
  Is he pursued?
GLOUCESTER
  Ay, my good lord.
CORNWALL
  If he be taken, he shall never more
  Be fear'd of doing harm: make your own purpose,
  How in my strength you please. For you, Edmund,
  Whose virtue and obedience doth this instant
  So much commend itself, you shall be ours:
  Natures of such deep trust we shall much need;
  You we first seize on.
EDMUND
  I shall serve you, sir,
  Truly, however else.
GLOUCESTER
  For him I thank your grace.
CORNWALL
  You know not why we came to visit you,--
REGAN
  Thus out of season, threading dark-eyed night:
  Occasions, noble Gloucester, of some poise,
  Wherein we must have use of your advice:
  Our father he hath writ, so hath our sister,
  Of differences, which I least thought it fit
  To answer from our home; the several messengers
  From hence attend dispatch. Our good old friend,
  Lay comforts to your bosom; and bestow
  Your needful counsel to our business,

Which craves the instant use.
GLOUCESTER
I serve you, madam:
Your graces are right welcome.

Exeunt

SCENE II.

Before Gloucester's castle.

Enter KENT and OSWALD, severally

OSWALD
Good dawning to thee, friend: art of this house?
KENT
Ay.
OSWALD
Where may we set our horses?
KENT
I' the mire.
OSWALD
Prithee, if thou lovest me, tell me.
KENT
I love thee not.
OSWALD
Why, then, I care not for thee.
KENT
If I had thee in Lipsbury pinfold, I would make thee
care for me.
OSWALD
Why dost thou use me thus? I know thee not.
KENT
Fellow, I know thee.
OSWALD
What dost thou know me for?

KENT

A knave; a rascal; an eater of broken meats; a
base, proud, shallow, beggarly, three-suited,
hundred-pound, filthy, worsted-stocking knave; a
lily-livered, action-taking knave, a whoreson,
glass-gazing, super-serviceable finical rogue;
one-trunk-inheriting slave; one that wouldst be a
bawd, in way of good service, and art nothing but
the composition of a knave, beggar, coward, pandar,
and the son and heir of a mongrel bitch: one whom I
will beat into clamorous whining, if thou deniest
the least syllable of thy addition.

OSWALD

Why, what a monstrous fellow art thou, thus to rail
on one that is neither known of thee nor knows thee!

KENT

What a brazen-faced varlet art thou, to deny thou
knowest me! Is it two days ago since I tripped up
thy heels, and beat thee before the king? Draw, you
rogue: for, though it be night, yet the moon
shines; I'll make a sop o' the moonshine of you:
draw, you whoreson cullionly barber-monger, draw.

Drawing his sword

OSWALD

Away! I have nothing to do with thee.

KENT

Draw, you rascal: you come with letters against the
king; and take vanity the puppet's part against the
royalty of her father: draw, you rogue, or I'll so
carbonado your shanks: draw, you rascal; come your
ways.

OSWALD

Help, ho! murder! help!

KENT

Strike, you slave; stand, rogue, stand; you neat
slave, strike.

Beating him

OSWALD

Help, ho! murder! murder!

*Enter EDMUND, with his rapier drawn, CORNWALL,
REGAN, GLOUCESTER, and Servants*

EDMUND

How now! What's the matter?

KENT

With you, goodman boy, an you please: come, I'll
flesh ye; come on, young master.

GLOUCESTER

Weapons! arms! What 's the matter here?

CORNWALL

Keep peace, upon your lives:

He dies that strikes again. What is the matter?

REGAN

The messengers from our sister and the king.

CORNWALL

What is your difference? speak.

OSWALD

I am scarce in breath, my lord.

KENT

No marvel, you have so bestirred your valour. You
cowardly rascal, nature disclaims in thee: a
tailor made thee.

CORNWALL

Thou art a strange fellow: a tailor make a man?

KENT

Ay, a tailor, sir: a stone-cutter or painter could
not have made him so ill, though he had been but two
hours at the trade.

CORNWALL

Speak yet, how grew your quarrel?

OSWALD

This ancient ruffian, sir, whose life I have spared
at suit of his gray beard,--

KENT

Thou whoreson zed! thou unnecessary letter! My
lord, if you will give me leave, I will tread this
unbolted villain into mortar, and daub the wall of
a jakes with him. Spare my gray beard, you wagtail?

CORNWALL

Peace, sirrah!
You beastly knave, know you no reverence?

KENT

Yes, sir; but anger hath a privilege.

CORNWALL

Why art thou angry?

KENT

That such a slave as this should wear a sword,
Who wears no honesty. Such smiling rogues as these,
Like rats, oft bite the holy cords a-twain
Which are too intrinse t' unloose; smooth every passion
That in the natures of their lords rebel;
Bring oil to fire, snow to their colder moods;
Renege, affirm, and turn their halcyon beaks
With every gale and vary of their masters,
Knowing nought, like dogs, but following.
A plague upon your epileptic visage!
Smile you my speeches, as I were a fool?
Goose, if I had you upon Sarum plain,
I'ld drive ye cackling home to Camelot.

CORNWALL

Why, art thou mad, old fellow?

GLOUCESTER

How fell you out? say that.

KENT

No contraries hold more antipathy

Than I and such a knave.

CORNWALL

Why dost thou call him a knave? What's his offence?

KENT

His countenance likes me not.

CORNWALL

No more, perchance, does mine, nor his, nor hers.

KENT

Sir, 'tis my occupation to be plain:

I have seen better faces in my time

Than stands on any shoulder that I see

Before me at this instant.

CORNWALL

This is some fellow,

Who, having been praised for bluntness, doth affect

A saucy roughness, and constrains the garb

Quite from his nature: he cannot flatter, he,

An honest mind and plain, he must speak truth!

An they will take it, so; if not, he's plain.

These kind of knaves I know, which in this plainness

Harbour more craft and more corrupter ends

Than twenty silly ducking observants

That stretch their duties nicely.

KENT

Sir, in good sooth, in sincere verity,

Under the allowance of your great aspect,

Whose influence, like the wreath of radiant fire

On flickering Phoebus' front,--

CORNWALL

What mean'st by this?

KENT

To go out of my dialect, which you
discommend so much. I know, sir, I am no
flatterer: he that beguiled you in a plain
accent was a plain knave; which for my part
I will not be, though I should win your displeasure
to entreat me to 't.

CORNWALL

What was the offence you gave him?

OSWALD

I never gave him any:
It pleased the king his master very late
To strike at me, upon his misconstruction;
When he, conjunct and flattering his displeasure,
Tripp'd me behind; being down, insulted, rail'd,
And put upon him such a deal of man,
That worthied him, got praises of the king
For him attempting who was self-subdued;
And, in the fleshment of this dread exploit,
Drew on me here again.

KENT

None of these rogues and cowards
But Ajax is their fool.

CORNWALL

Fetch forth the stocks!
You stubborn ancient knave, you reverend braggart,
We'll teach you--

KENT

Sir, I am too old to learn:
Call not your stocks for me: I serve the king;
On whose employment I was sent to you:
You shall do small respect, show too bold malice

Against the grace and person of my master,
Stocking his messenger.

CORNWALL

Fetch forth the stocks! As I have life and honour,
There shall he sit till noon.

REGAN

Till noon! till night, my lord; and all night too.

KENT

Why, madam, if I were your father's dog,
You should not use me so.

REGAN

Sir, being his knave, I will.

CORNWALL

This is a fellow of the self-same colour
Our sister speaks of. Come, bring away the stocks!

Stocks brought out

GLOUCESTER

Let me beseech your grace not to do so:
His fault is much, and the good king his master
Will cheque him for 't: your purposed low correction
Is such as basest and contemned'st wretches
For pilferings and most common trespasses
Are punish'd with: the king must take it ill,
That he's so slightly valued in his messenger,
Should have him thus restrain'd.

CORNWALL

I'll answer that.

REGAN

My sister may receive it much more worse,
To have her gentleman abused, assaulted,
For following her affairs. Put in his legs.

KENT is put in the stocks

Come, my good lord, away.

Exeunt all but GLOUCESTER and KENT

GLOUCESTER

    I am sorry for thee, friend; 'tis the duke's pleasure,
    Whose disposition, all the world well knows,
    Will not be rubb'd nor stopp'd: I'll entreat for thee.

KENT

    Pray, do not, sir: I have watched and travell'd hard;
    Some time I shall sleep out, the rest I'll whistle.
    A good man's fortune may grow out at heels:
    Give you good morrow!

GLOUCESTER

    The duke's to blame in this; 'twill be ill taken.

Exit

KENT

    Good king, that must approve the common saw,
    Thou out of heaven's benediction comest
    To the warm sun!
    Approach, thou beacon to this under globe,
    That by thy comfortable beams I may
    Peruse this letter! Nothing almost sees miracles
    But misery: I know 'tis from Cordelia,
    Who hath most fortunately been inform'd
    Of my obscured course; and shall find time
    From this enormous state, seeking to give
    Losses their remedies. All weary and o'erwatch'd,
    Take vantage, heavy eyes, not to behold
    This shameful lodging.
    Fortune, good night: smile once more: turn thy wheel!

Sleeps

SCENE III.

A wood.

Enter EDGAR

EDGAR
    I heard myself proclaim'd;
    And by the happy hollow of a tree
    Escaped the hunt. No port is free; no place,
    That guard, and most unusual vigilance,
    Does not attend my taking. Whiles I may 'scape,
    I will preserve myself: and am bethought
    To take the basest and most poorest shape
    That ever penury, in contempt of man,
    Brought near to beast: my face I'll grime with filth;
    Blanket my loins: elf all my hair in knots;
    And with presented nakedness out-face
    The winds and persecutions of the sky.
    The country gives me proof and precedent
    Of Bedlam beggars, who, with roaring voices,
    Strike in their numb'd and mortified bare arms
    Pins, wooden pricks, nails, sprigs of rosemary;
    And with this horrible object, from low farms,
    Poor pelting villages, sheep-cotes, and mills,
    Sometime with lunatic bans, sometime with prayers,
    Enforce their charity. Poor Turlygod! poor Tom!
    That's something yet: Edgar I nothing am.

Exit

SCENE IV.

Before GLOUCESTER's castle. KENT in the stocks.

Enter KING LEAR, Fool, and Gentleman

KING LEAR

'Tis strange that they should so depart from home,
And not send back my messenger.

Gentleman

As I learn'd,
The night before there was no purpose in them
Of this remove.

KENT

Hail to thee, noble master!

KING LEAR

Ha!
Makest thou this shame thy pastime?

KENT

No, my lord.

Fool

Ha, ha! he wears cruel garters. Horses are tied
by the heads, dogs and bears by the neck, monkeys by
the loins, and men by the legs: when a man's
over-lusty at legs, then he wears wooden
nether-stocks.

KING LEAR

What's he that hath so much thy place mistook
To set thee here?

KENT

It is both he and she;
Your son and daughter.

KING LEAR

No.

KENT

Yes.

KING LEAR

No, I say.

KENT

I say, yea.

KING LEAR

No, no, they would not.

KENT

Yes, they have.

KING LEAR

By Jupiter, I swear, no.

KENT

By Juno, I swear, ay.

KING LEAR

They durst not do 't;
They could not, would not do 't; 'tis worse than murder,
To do upon respect such violent outrage:
Resolve me, with all modest haste, which way
Thou mightst deserve, or they impose, this usage,
Coming from us.

KENT

My lord, when at their home
I did commend your highness' letters to them,
Ere I was risen from the place that show'd
My duty kneeling, came there a reeking post,
Stew'd in his haste, half breathless, panting forth
From Goneril his mistress salutations;
Deliver'd letters, spite of intermission,
Which presently they read: on whose contents,
They summon'd up their meiny, straight took horse;
Commanded me to follow, and attend
The leisure of their answer; gave me cold looks:
And meeting here the other messenger,
Whose welcome, I perceived, had poison'd mine,--
Being the very fellow that of late
Display'd so saucily against your highness,--
Having more man than wit about me, drew:
He raised the house with loud and coward cries.
Your son and daughter found this trespass worth
The shame which here it suffers.

Fool

    Winter's not gone yet, if the wild-geese fly that way.
    Fathers that wear rags
    Do make their children blind;
    But fathers that bear bags
    Shall see their children kind.
    Fortune, that arrant whore,
    Ne'er turns the key to the poor.
    But, for all this, thou shalt have as many dolours
    for thy daughters as thou canst tell in a year.

KING LEAR

    O, how this mother swells up toward my heart!
    Hysterica passio, down, thou climbing sorrow,
    Thy element's below! Where is this daughter?

KENT

    With the earl, sir, here within.

KING LEAR

    Follow me not;
    Stay here.

Exit

Gentleman

    Made you no more offence but what you speak of?

KENT

    None.
    How chance the king comes with so small a train?

Fool

    And thou hadst been set i' the stocks for that
    question, thou hadst well deserved it.

KENT

    Why, fool?

Fool

    We'll set thee to school to an ant, to teach thee
    there's no labouring i' the winter. All that follow

their noses are led by their eyes but blind men; and
there's not a nose among twenty but can smell him
that's stinking. Let go thy hold when a great wheel
runs down a hill, lest it break thy neck with
following it: but the great one that goes up the
hill, let him draw thee after. When a wise man
gives thee better counsel, give me mine again: I
would have none but knaves follow it, since a fool gives
it.
That sir which serves and seeks for gain,
And follows but for form,
Will pack when it begins to rain,
And leave thee in the storm,
But I will tarry; the fool will stay,
And let the wise man fly:
The knave turns fool that runs away;
The fool no knave, perdy.

KENT

Where learned you this, fool?

Fool

Not i' the stocks, fool.

Re-enter KING LEAR with GLOUCESTER

KING LEAR

Deny to speak with me? They are sick? they are weary?
They have travell'd all the night? Mere fetches;
The images of revolt and flying off.
Fetch me a better answer.

GLOUCESTER

My dear lord,
You know the fiery quality of the duke;
How unremoveable and fix'd he is
In his own course.

KING LEAR

Vengeance! plague! death! confusion!
Fiery? what quality? Why, Gloucester, Gloucester,
I'ld speak with the Duke of Cornwall and his wife.
GLOUCESTER
Well, my good lord, I have inform'd them so.
KING LEAR
Inform'd them! Dost thou understand me, man?
GLOUCESTER
Ay, my good lord.
KING LEAR
The king would speak with Cornwall; the dear father
Would with his daughter speak, commands her service:
Are they inform'd of this? My breath and blood!
Fiery? the fiery duke? Tell the hot duke that--
No, but not yet: may be he is not well:
Infirmity doth still neglect all office
Whereto our health is bound; we are not ourselves
When nature, being oppress'd, commands the mind
To suffer with the body: I'll forbear;
And am fall'n out with my more headier will,
To take the indisposed and sickly fit
For the sound man. Death on my state! wherefore

Looking on KENT

Should he sit here? This act persuades me
That this remotion of the duke and her
Is practise only. Give me my servant forth.
Go tell the duke and 's wife I'ld speak with them,
Now, presently: bid them come forth and hear me,
Or at their chamber-door I'll beat the drum
Till it cry sleep to death.
GLOUCESTER
I would have all well betwixt you.

Exit

KING LEAR

O me, my heart, my rising heart! but, down!

Fool

Cry to it, nuncle, as the cockney did to the eels
when she put 'em i' the paste alive; she knapped 'em
o' the coxcombs with a stick, and cried 'Down,
wantons, down!' 'Twas her brother that, in pure
kindness to his horse, buttered his hay.

Enter CORNWALL, REGAN, GLOUCESTER, and Servants

KING LEAR

Good morrow to you both.

CORNWALL

Hail to your grace!

KENT is set at liberty

REGAN

I am glad to see your highness.

KING LEAR

Regan, I think you are; I know what reason
I have to think so: if thou shouldst not be glad,
I would divorce me from thy mother's tomb,
Sepulchring an adultress.

To KENT

O, are you free?
Some other time for that. Beloved Regan,
Thy sister's naught: O Regan, she hath tied
Sharp-tooth'd unkindness, like a vulture, here:
Points to his heart

I can scarce speak to thee; thou'lt not believe
With how depraved a quality--O Regan!
REGAN

I pray you, sir, take patience: I have hope.
You less know how to value her desert
Than she to scant her duty.
KING LEAR

Say, how is that?
REGAN

I cannot think my sister in the least
Would fail her obligation: if, sir, perchance
She have restrain'd the riots of your followers,
'Tis on such ground, and to such wholesome end,
As clears her from all blame.
KING LEAR

My curses on her!
REGAN

O, sir, you are old.
Nature in you stands on the very verge
Of her confine: you should be ruled and led
By some discretion, that discerns your state
Better than you yourself. Therefore, I pray you,
That to our sister you do make return;
Say you have wrong'd her, sir.
KING LEAR

Ask her forgiveness?
Do you but mark how this becomes the house:
'Dear daughter, I confess that I am old;

Kneeling

Age is unnecessary: on my knees I beg
That you'll vouchsafe me raiment, bed, and food.'
REGAN

Good sir, no more; these are unsightly tricks:

Return you to my sister.

KING LEAR

[Rising] Never, Regan:
She hath abated me of half my train;
Look'd black upon me; struck me with her tongue,
Most serpent-like, upon the very heart:
All the stored vengeances of heaven fall
On her ingrateful top! Strike her young bones,
You taking airs, with lameness!

CORNWALL

Fie, sir, fie!

KING LEAR

You nimble lightnings, dart your blinding flames
Into her scornful eyes! Infect her beauty,
You fen-suck'd fogs, drawn by the powerful sun,
To fall and blast her pride!

REGAN

O the blest gods! so will you wish on me,
When the rash mood is on.

KING LEAR

No, Regan, thou shalt never have my curse:
Thy tender-hefted nature shall not give
Thee o'er to harshness: her eyes are fierce; but thine
Do comfort and not burn. 'Tis not in thee
To grudge my pleasures, to cut off my train,
To bandy hasty words, to scant my sizes,
And in conclusion to oppose the bolt
Against my coming in: thou better know'st
The offices of nature, bond of childhood,
Effects of courtesy, dues of gratitude;
Thy half o' the kingdom hast thou not forgot,
Wherein I thee endow'd.

REGAN

Good sir, to the purpose.

KING LEAR
  Who put my man i' the stocks?

Tucket within

CORNWALL
  What trumpet's that?
REGAN
  I know't, my sister's: this approves her letter,
  That she would soon be here.

Enter OSWALD

  Is your lady come?
KING LEAR
  This is a slave, whose easy-borrow'd pride
  Dwells in the fickle grace of her he follows.
  Out, varlet, from my sight!
CORNWALL
  What means your grace?
KING LEAR
  Who stock'd my servant? Regan, I have good hope
  Thou didst not know on't. Who comes here? O heavens,

Enter GONERIL

  If you do love old men, if your sweet sway
  Allow obedience, if yourselves are old,
  Make it your cause; send down, and take my part!

To GONERIL

  Art not ashamed to look upon this beard?
  O Regan, wilt thou take her by the hand?
GONERIL
  Why not by the hand, sir? How have I offended?
  All's not offence that indiscretion finds

And dotage terms so.
KING LEAR
  O sides, you are too tough;
  Will you yet hold? How came my man i' the stocks?
CORNWALL
  I set him there, sir: but his own disorders
  Deserved much less advancement.
KING LEAR
  You! did you?
REGAN
  I pray you, father, being weak, seem so.
  If, till the expiration of your month,
  You will return and sojourn with my sister,
  Dismissing half your train, come then to me:
  I am now from home, and out of that provision
  Which shall be needful for your entertainment.
KING LEAR
  Return to her, and fifty men dismiss'd?
  No, rather I abjure all roofs, and choose
  To wage against the enmity o' the air;
  To be a comrade with the wolf and owl,--
  Necessity's sharp pinch! Return with her?
  Why, the hot-blooded France, that dowerless took
  Our youngest born, I could as well be brought
  To knee his throne, and, squire-like; pension beg
  To keep base life afoot. Return with her?
  Persuade me rather to be slave and sumpter
  To this detested groom.

        Pointing at OSWALD

GONERIL
  At your choice, sir.
KING LEAR
  I prithee, daughter, do not make me mad:

I will not trouble thee, my child; farewell:
We'll no more meet, no more see one another:
But yet thou art my flesh, my blood, my daughter;
Or rather a disease that's in my flesh,
Which I must needs call mine: thou art a boil,
A plague-sore, an embossed carbuncle,
In my corrupted blood. But I'll not chide thee;
Let shame come when it will, I do not call it:
I do not bid the thunder-bearer shoot,
Nor tell tales of thee to high-judging Jove:
Mend when thou canst; be better at thy leisure:
I can be patient; I can stay with Regan,
I and my hundred knights.

REGAN

Not altogether so:
I look'd not for you yet, nor am provided
For your fit welcome. Give ear, sir, to my sister;
For those that mingle reason with your passion
Must be content to think you old, and so--
But she knows what she does.

KING LEAR

Is this well spoken?

REGAN

I dare avouch it, sir: what, fifty followers?
Is it not well? What should you need of more?
Yea, or so many, sith that both charge and danger
Speak 'gainst so great a number? How, in one house,
Should many people, under two commands,
Hold amity? 'Tis hard; almost impossible.

GONERIL

Why might not you, my lord, receive attendance
From those that she calls servants or from mine?

REGAN

Why not, my lord? If then they chanced to slack you,

We could control them. If you will come to me,--
For now I spy a danger,--I entreat you
To bring but five and twenty: to no more
Will I give place or notice.
KING LEAR
I gave you all--
REGAN
And in good time you gave it.
KING LEAR
Made you my guardians, my depositaries;
But kept a reservation to be follow'd
With such a number. What, must I come to you
With five and twenty, Regan? said you so?
REGAN
And speak't again, my lord; no more with me.
KING LEAR
Those wicked creatures yet do look well-favour'd,
When others are more wicked: not being the worst
Stands in some rank of praise.

To GONERIL

I'll go with thee:
Thy fifty yet doth double five and twenty,
And thou art twice her love.
GONERIL
Hear me, my lord;
What need you five and twenty, ten, or five,
To follow in a house where twice so many
Have a command to tend you?
REGAN
What need one?
KING LEAR
O, reason not the need: our basest beggars
Are in the poorest thing superfluous:

Allow not nature more than nature needs,
Man's life's as cheap as beast's: thou art a lady;
If only to go warm were gorgeous,
Why, nature needs not what thou gorgeous wear'st,
Which scarcely keeps thee warm. But, for true need,--
You heavens, give me that patience, patience I need!
You see me here, you gods, a poor old man,
As full of grief as age; wretched in both!
If it be you that stir these daughters' hearts
Against their father, fool me not so much
To bear it tamely; touch me with noble anger,
And let not women's weapons, water-drops,
Stain my man's cheeks! No, you unnatural hags,
I will have such revenges on you both,
That all the world shall--I will do such things,--
What they are, yet I know not: but they shall be
The terrors of the earth. You think I'll weep
No, I'll not weep:
I have full cause of weeping; but this heart
Shall break into a hundred thousand flaws,
Or ere I'll weep. O fool, I shall go mad!

Exeunt KING LEAR, GLOUCESTER, KENT, and Fool

Storm and tempest

CORNWALL
Let us withdraw; 'twill be a storm.
REGAN
This house is little: the old man and his people
Cannot be well bestow'd.
GONERIL
'Tis his own blame; hath put himself from rest,
And must needs taste his folly.
REGAN

For his particular, I'll receive him gladly,
But not one follower.

GONERIL

So am I purposed.
Where is my lord of Gloucester?

CORNWALL

Follow'd the old man forth: he is return'd.

Re-enter GLOUCESTER

GLOUCESTER

The king is in high rage.

CORNWALL

Whither is he going?

GLOUCESTER

He calls to horse; but will I know not whither.

CORNWALL

'Tis best to give him way; he leads himself.

GONERIL

My lord, entreat him by no means to stay.

GLOUCESTER

Alack, the night comes on, and the bleak winds
Do sorely ruffle; for many miles a bout
There's scarce a bush.

REGAN

O, sir, to wilful men,
The injuries that they themselves procure
Must be their schoolmasters. Shut up your doors:
He is attended with a desperate train;
And what they may incense him to, being apt
To have his ear abused, wisdom bids fear.

CORNWALL

Shut up your doors, my lord; 'tis a wild night:
My Regan counsels well; come out o' the storm.

Exeunt

75

ACT III

SCENE I.

A heath.

Storm still. Enter KENT and a Gentleman, meeting

KENT
  Who's there, besides foul weather?
Gentleman
  One minded like the weather, most unquietly.
KENT
  I know you. Where's the king?
Gentleman
  Contending with the fretful element:
  Bids the winds blow the earth into the sea,
  Or swell the curled water 'bove the main,
  That things might change or cease; tears his white hair,
  Which the impetuous blasts, with eyeless rage,
  Catch in their fury, and make nothing of;
  Strives in his little world of man to out-scorn
  The to-and-fro-conflicting wind and rain.
  This night, wherein the cub-drawn bear would couch,
  The lion and the belly-pinched wolf
  Keep their fur dry, unbonneted he runs,
  And bids what will take all.
KENT
  But who is with him?
Gentleman
  None but the fool; who labours to out-jest
  His heart-struck injuries.
KENT
  Sir, I do know you;
  And dare, upon the warrant of my note,

Commend a dear thing to you. There is division,
Although as yet the face of it be cover'd
With mutual cunning, 'twixt Albany and Cornwall;
Who have--as who have not, that their great stars
Throned and set high?--servants, who seem no less,
Which are to France the spies and speculations
Intelligent of our state; what hath been seen,
Either in snuffs and packings of the dukes,
Or the hard rein which both of them have borne
Against the old kind king; or something deeper,
Whereof perchance these are but furnishings;
But, true it is, from France there comes a power
Into this scatter'd kingdom; who already,
Wise in our negligence, have secret feet
In some of our best ports, and are at point
To show their open banner. Now to you:
If on my credit you dare build so far
To make your speed to Dover, you shall find
Some that will thank you, making just report
Of how unnatural and bemadding sorrow
The king hath cause to plain.
I am a gentleman of blood and breeding;
And, from some knowledge and assurance, offer
This office to you.

Gentleman

I will talk further with you.

KENT

No, do not.
For confirmation that I am much more
Than my out-wall, open this purse, and take
What it contains. If you shall see Cordelia,--
As fear not but you shall,--show her this ring;
And she will tell you who your fellow is
That yet you do not know. Fie on this storm!

I will go seek the king.
Gentleman
    Give me your hand: have you no more to say?
KENT
    Few words, but, to effect, more than all yet;
    That, when we have found the king,--in which your pain
    That way, I'll this,--he that first lights on him
    Holla the other.

Exeunt severally

SCENE II.

Another part of the heath. Storm still.

Enter KING LEAR and Fool

KING LEAR
    Blow, winds, and crack your cheeks! rage! blow!
    You cataracts and hurricanoes, spout
    Till you have drench'd our steeples, drown'd the cocks!
    You sulphurous and thought-executing fires,
    Vaunt-couriers to oak-cleaving thunderbolts,
    Singe my white head! And thou, all-shaking thunder,
    Smite flat the thick rotundity o' the world!
    Crack nature's moulds, an germens spill at once,
    That make ingrateful man!
Fool
    O nuncle, court holy-water in a dry
    house is better than this rain-water out o' door.
    Good nuncle, in, and ask thy daughters' blessing:
    here's a night pities neither wise man nor fool.
KING LEAR
    Rumble thy bellyful! Spit, fire! spout, rain!
    Nor rain, wind, thunder, fire, are my daughters:
    I tax not you, you elements, with unkindness;

I never gave you kingdom, call'd you children,
You owe me no subscription: then let fall
Your horrible pleasure: here I stand, your slave,
A poor, infirm, weak, and despised old man:
But yet I call you servile ministers,
That have with two pernicious daughters join'd
Your high engender'd battles 'gainst a head
So old and white as this. O! O! 'tis foul!

Fool

He that has a house to put's head in has a good
head-piece.
The cod-piece that will house
Before the head has any,
The head and he shall louse;
So beggars marry many.
The man that makes his toe
What he his heart should make
Shall of a corn cry woe,
And turn his sleep to wake.
For there was never yet fair woman but she made
mouths in a glass.

KING LEAR

No, I will be the pattern of all patience;
I will say nothing.

Enter KENT

KENT

Who's there?

Fool

Marry, here's grace and a cod-piece; that's a wise
man and a fool.

KENT

Alas, sir, are you here? things that love night
Love not such nights as these; the wrathful skies

Gallow the very wanderers of the dark,
And make them keep their caves: since I was man,
Such sheets of fire, such bursts of horrid thunder,
Such groans of roaring wind and rain, I never
Remember to have heard: man's nature cannot carry
The affliction nor the fear.

KING LEAR

Let the great gods,
That keep this dreadful pother o'er our heads,
Find out their enemies now. Tremble, thou wretch,
That hast within thee undivulged crimes,
Unwhipp'd of justice: hide thee, thou bloody hand;
Thou perjured, and thou simular man of virtue
That art incestuous: caitiff, to pieces shake,
That under covert and convenient seeming
Hast practised on man's life: close pent-up guilts,
Rive your concealing continents, and cry
These dreadful summoners grace. I am a man
More sinn'd against than sinning.

KENT

Alack, bare-headed!
Gracious my lord, hard by here is a hovel;
Some friendship will it lend you 'gainst the tempest:
Repose you there; while I to this hard house--
More harder than the stones whereof 'tis raised;
Which even but now, demanding after you,
Denied me to come in--return, and force
Their scanted courtesy.

KING LEAR

My wits begin to turn.
Come on, my boy: how dost, my boy? art cold?
I am cold myself. Where is this straw, my fellow?
The art of our necessities is strange,
That can make vile things precious. Come,

80

your hovel.
Poor fool and knave, I have one part in my heart
That's sorry yet for thee.

Fool

[Singing]
He that has and a little tiny wit--
With hey, ho, the wind and the rain,--
Must make content with his fortunes fit,
For the rain it raineth every day.

KING LEAR

True, my good boy. Come, bring us to this hovel.

Exeunt KING LEAR and KENT

Fool

This is a brave night to cool a courtezan.
I'll speak a prophecy ere I go:
When priests are more in word than matter;
When brewers mar their malt with water;
When nobles are their tailors' tutors;
No heretics burn'd, but wenches' suitors;
When every case in law is right;
No squire in debt, nor no poor knight;
When slanders do not live in tongues;
Nor cutpurses come not to throngs;
When usurers tell their gold i' the field;
And bawds and whores do churches build;
Then shall the realm of Albion
Come to great confusion:
Then comes the time, who lives to see't,
That going shall be used with feet.
This prophecy Merlin shall make; for I live before his
time.

Exit

SCENE III.

Gloucester's castle.

Enter GLOUCESTER and EDMUND

GLOUCESTER

Alack, alack, Edmund, I like not this unnatural
dealing. When I desire their leave that I might
pity him, they took from me the use of mine own
house; charged me, on pain of their perpetual
displeasure, neither to speak of him, entreat for
him, nor any way sustain him.

EDMUND

Most savage and unnatural!

GLOUCESTER

Go to; say you nothing. There's a division betwixt
the dukes; and a worse matter than that: I have
received a letter this night; 'tis dangerous to be
spoken; I have locked the letter in my closet:
these injuries the king now bears will be revenged
home; there's part of a power already footed: we
must incline to the king. I will seek him, and
privily relieve him: go you and maintain talk with
the duke, that my charity be not of him perceived:
if he ask for me. I am ill, and gone to bed.
Though I die for it, as no less is threatened me,
the king my old master must be relieved. There is
some strange thing toward, Edmund; pray you, be
careful.

Exit

EDMUND

This courtesy, forbid thee, shall the duke

82

Instantly know; and of that letter too:
This seems a fair deserving, and must draw me
That which my father loses; no less than all:
The younger rises when the old doth fall.

Exit

SCENE IV.

The heath. Before a hovel.

Enter KING LEAR, KENT, and Fool

KENT

Here is the place, my lord; good my lord, enter:
The tyranny of the open night's too rough
For nature to endure.

Storm still

KING LEAR

Let me alone.

KENT

Good my lord, enter here.

KING LEAR

Wilt break my heart?

KENT

I had rather break mine own. Good my lord, enter.

KING LEAR

Thou think'st 'tis much that this contentious storm
Invades us to the skin: so 'tis to thee;
But where the greater malady is fix'd,
The lesser is scarce felt. Thou'ldst shun a bear;
But if thy flight lay toward the raging sea,
Thou'ldst meet the bear i' the mouth. When the
mind's free,

The body's delicate: the tempest in my mind
Doth from my senses take all feeling else
Save what beats there. Filial ingratitude!
Is it not as this mouth should tear this hand
For lifting food to't? But I will punish home:
No, I will weep no more. In such a night
To shut me out! Pour on; I will endure.
In such a night as this! O Regan, Goneril!
Your old kind father, whose frank heart gave all,--
O, that way madness lies; let me shun that;
No more of that.

KENT

Good my lord, enter here.

KING LEAR

Prithee, go in thyself: seek thine own ease:
This tempest will not give me leave to ponder
On things would hurt me more. But I'll go in.

To the Fool

In, boy; go first. You houseless poverty,--
Nay, get thee in. I'll pray, and then I'll sleep.

Fool goes in

Poor naked wretches, whereso'er you are,
That bide the pelting of this pitiless storm,
How shall your houseless heads and unfed sides,
Your loop'd and window'd raggedness, defend you
From seasons such as these? O, I have ta'en
Too little care of this! Take physic, pomp;
Expose thyself to feel what wretches feel,
That thou mayst shake the superflux to them,
And show the heavens more just.

EDGAR

[Within] Fathom and half, fathom and half! Poor Tom!

The Fool runs out from the hovel

Fool

Come not in here, nuncle, here's a spirit
Help me, help me!

KENT

Give me thy hand. Who's there?

Fool

A spirit, a spirit: he says his name's poor Tom.

KENT

What art thou that dost grumble there i' the straw?
Come forth.

Enter EDGAR disguised as a mad man

EDGAR

Away! the foul fiend follows me!
Through the sharp hawthorn blows the cold wind.
Hum! go to thy cold bed, and warm thee.

KING LEAR

Hast thou given all to thy two daughters?
And art thou come to this?

EDGAR

Who gives any thing to poor Tom? whom the foul
fiend hath led through fire and through flame, and
through ford and whirlipool e'er bog and quagmire;
that hath laid knives under his pillow, and halters
in his pew; set ratsbane by his porridge; made film
proud of heart, to ride on a bay trotting-horse over
four-inched bridges, to course his own shadow for a
traitor. Bless thy five wits! Tom's a-cold,--O, do
de, do de, do de. Bless thee from whirlwinds,
star-blasting, and taking! Do poor Tom some

charity, whom the foul fiend vexes: there could I
have him now,--and there,--and there again, and there.

Storm still

KING LEAR

What, have his daughters brought him to this pass?
Couldst thou save nothing? Didst thou give them all?
Fool

Nay, he reserved a blanket, else we had been all shamed.
KING LEAR

Now, all the plagues that in the pendulous air
Hang fated o'er men's faults light on thy daughters!
KENT

He hath no daughters, sir.
KING LEAR

Death, traitor! nothing could have subdued nature
To such a lowness but his unkind daughters.
Is it the fashion, that discarded fathers
Should have thus little mercy on their flesh?
Judicious punishment! 'twas this flesh begot
Those pelican daughters.
EDGAR

Pillicock sat on Pillicock-hill:
Halloo, halloo, loo, loo!
Fool

This cold night will turn us all to fools and madmen.
EDGAR

Take heed o' the foul fiend: obey thy parents;
keep thy word justly; swear not; commit not with
man's sworn spouse; set not thy sweet heart on proud
array. Tom's a-cold.
KING LEAR

What hast thou been?
EDGAR

A serving-man, proud in heart and mind; that curled
my hair; wore gloves in my cap; served the lust of
my mistress' heart, and did the act of darkness with
her; swore as many oaths as I spake words, and
broke them in the sweet face of heaven: one that
slept in the contriving of lust, and waked to do it:
wine loved I deeply, dice dearly: and in woman
out-paramoured the Turk: false of heart, light of
ear, bloody of hand; hog in sloth, fox in stealth,
wolf in greediness, dog in madness, lion in prey.
Let not the creaking of shoes nor the rustling of
silks betray thy poor heart to woman: keep thy foot
out of brothels, thy hand out of plackets, thy pen
from lenders' books, and defy the foul fiend.
Still through the hawthorn blows the cold wind:
Says suum, mun, ha, no, nonny.
Dolphin my boy, my boy, sessa! let him trot by.

Storm still

KING LEAR
Why, thou wert better in thy grave than to answer
with thy uncovered body this extremity of the skies.
Is man no more than this? Consider him well. Thou
owest the worm no silk, the beast no hide, the sheep
no wool, the cat no perfume. Ha! here's three on
's are sophisticated! Thou art the thing itself:
unaccommodated man is no more but such a poor bare,
forked animal as thou art. Off, off, you lendings!
come unbutton here.

Tearing off his clothes

Fool
Prithee, nuncle, be contented; 'tis a naughty night

to swim in. Now a little fire in a wild field were
like an old lecher's heart; a small spark, all the
rest on's body cold. Look, here comes a walking fire.

Enter GLOUCESTER, with a torch

EDGAR

This is the foul fiend Flibbertigibbet: he begins
at curfew, and walks till the first cock; he gives
the web and the pin, squints the eye, and makes the
hare-lip; mildews the white wheat, and hurts the
poor creature of earth.
S. Withold footed thrice the old;
He met the night-mare, and her nine-fold;
Bid her alight,
And her troth plight,
And, aroint thee, witch, aroint thee!

KENT

How fares your grace?

KING LEAR

What's he?

KENT

Who's there? What is't you seek?

GLOUCESTER

What are you there? Your names?

EDGAR

Poor Tom; that eats the swimming frog, the toad,
the tadpole, the wall-newt and the water; that in
the fury of his heart, when the foul fiend rages,
eats cow-dung for sallets; swallows the old rat and
the ditch-dog; drinks the green mantle of the
standing pool; who is whipped from tithing to
tithing, and stock- punished, and imprisoned; who
hath had three suits to his back, six shirts to his
body, horse to ride, and weapon to wear;

But mice and rats, and such small deer,
Have been Tom's food for seven long year.
Beware my follower. Peace, Smulkin; peace, thou fiend!
GLOUCESTER
What, hath your grace no better company?
EDGAR
The prince of darkness is a gentleman:
Modo he's call'd, and Mahu.
GLOUCESTER
Our flesh and blood is grown so vile, my lord,
That it doth hate what gets it.
EDGAR
Poor Tom's a-cold.
GLOUCESTER
Go in with me: my duty cannot suffer
To obey in all your daughters' hard commands:
Though their injunction be to bar my doors,
And let this tyrannous night take hold upon you,
Yet have I ventured to come seek you out,
And bring you where both fire and food is ready.
KING LEAR
First let me talk with this philosopher.
What is the cause of thunder?
KENT
Good my lord, take his offer; go into the house.
KING LEAR
I'll talk a word with this same learned Theban.
What is your study?
EDGAR
How to prevent the fiend, and to kill vermin.
KING LEAR
Let me ask you one word in private.
KENT
Importune him once more to go, my lord;

His wits begin to unsettle.
GLOUCESTER
  Canst thou blame him?

  Storm still

  His daughters seek his death: ah, that good Kent!
  He said it would be thus, poor banish'd man!
  Thou say'st the king grows mad; I'll tell thee, friend,
  I am almost mad myself: I had a son,
  Now outlaw'd from my blood; he sought my life,
  But lately, very late: I loved him, friend;
  No father his son dearer: truth to tell thee,
  The grief hath crazed my wits. What a night's this!
  I do beseech your grace,--
KING LEAR
  O, cry your mercy, sir.
  Noble philosopher, your company.
EDGAR
  Tom's a-cold.
GLOUCESTER
  In, fellow, there, into the hovel: keep thee warm.
KING LEAR
  Come let's in all.
KENT
  This way, my lord.
KING LEAR
  With him;
  I will keep still with my philosopher.
KENT
  Good my lord, soothe him; let him take the fellow.
GLOUCESTER
  Take him you on.
KENT
  Sirrah, come on; go along with us.

KING LEAR

Come, good Athenian.

GLOUCESTER

No words, no words: hush.

EDGAR

Child Rowland to the dark tower came,
His word was still,--Fie, foh, and fum,
I smell the blood of a British man.

Exeunt

SCENE V.

Gloucester's castle.

Enter CORNWALL and EDMUND

CORNWALL

I will have my revenge ere I depart his house.

EDMUND

How, my lord, I may be censured, that nature thus
gives way to loyalty, something fears me to think
of.

CORNWALL

I now perceive, it was not altogether your
brother's evil disposition made him seek his death;
but a provoking merit, set a-work by a reprovable
badness in himself.

EDMUND

How malicious is my fortune, that I must repent to
be just! This is the letter he spoke of, which
approves him an intelligent party to the advantages
of France: O heavens! that this treason were not,
or not I the detector!

CORNWALL

o with me to the duchess.

EDMUND

    If the matter of this paper be certain, you have
    mighty business in hand.

CORNWALL

    True or false, it hath made thee earl of
    Gloucester. Seek out where thy father is, that he
    may be ready for our apprehension.

EDMUND

    [Aside] If I find him comforting the king, it will
    stuff his suspicion more fully.--I will persevere in
    my course of loyalty, though the conflict be sore
    between that and my blood.

CORNWALL

    I will lay trust upon thee; and thou shalt find a
    dearer father in my love.

Exeunt

SCENE VI.

A chamber in a farmhouse adjoining the castle.

*Enter GLOUCESTER, KING LEAR, KENT, Fool, and
EDGAR*

GLOUCESTER

    Here is better than the open air; take it
    thankfully. I will piece out the comfort with what
    addition I can: I will not be long from you.

KENT

    All the power of his wits have given way to his
    impatience: the gods reward your kindness!

Exit GLOUCESTER

EDGAR

    Frateretto calls me; and tells me

Nero is an angler in the lake of darkness.
Pray, innocent, and beware the foul fiend.

Fool

Prithee, nuncle, tell me whether a madman be a
gentleman or a yeoman?

KING LEAR

A king, a king!

Fool

No, he's a yeoman that has a gentleman to his son;
for he's a mad yeoman that sees his son a gentleman
before him.

KING LEAR

To have a thousand with red burning spits
Come hissing in upon 'em,--

EDGAR

The foul fiend bites my back.

Fool

He's mad that trusts in the tameness of a wolf, a
horse's health, a boy's love, or a whore's oath.

KING LEAR

It shall be done; I will arraign them straight.

To EDGAR

Come, sit thou here, most learned justicer;

To the Fool

Thou, sapient sir, sit here. Now, you she foxes!

EDGAR

Look, where he stands and glares!
Wantest thou eyes at trial, madam?
Come o'er the bourn, Bessy, to me,--

Fool

Her boat hath a leak,

And she must not speak
Why she dares not come over to thee.
KENT

EDGAR

The foul fiend haunts poor Tom in the voice of a
nightingale. Hopdance cries in Tom's belly for two
white herring. Croak not, black angel; I have no
food for thee.
KENT

How do you, sir? Stand you not so amazed:
Will you lie down and rest upon the cushions?
KING LEAR

I'll see their trial first. Bring in the evidence.

To EDGAR

Thou robed man of justice, take thy place;

To the Fool

And thou, his yoke-fellow of equity,
Bench by his side:

To KENT

you are o' the commission,
Sit you too.
EDGAR

Let us deal justly.
Sleepest or wakest thou, jolly shepherd?
Thy sheep be in the corn;
And for one blast of thy minikin mouth,
Thy sheep shall take no harm.
Pur! the cat is gray.
KING LEAR

Arraign her first; 'tis Goneril. I here take my
oath before this honourable assembly, she kicked the

poor king her father.

Fool

Come hither, mistress. Is your name Goneril?

KING LEAR

She cannot deny it.

Fool

Cry you mercy, I took you for a joint-stool.

KING LEAR

And here's another, whose warp'd looks proclaim
What store her heart is made on. Stop her there!
Arms, arms, sword, fire! Corruption in the place!
False justicer, why hast thou let her 'scape?

EDGAR

Bless thy five wits!

KENT

O pity! Sir, where is the patience now,
That thou so oft have boasted to retain?

EDGAR

[Aside] My tears begin to take his part so much,
They'll mar my counterfeiting.

KING LEAR

The little dogs and all, Tray, Blanch, and
Sweet-heart, see, they bark at me.

EDGAR

Tom will throw his head at them. Avaunt, you curs!
Be thy mouth or black or white,
Tooth that poisons if it bite;
Mastiff, grey-hound, mongrel grim,
Hound or spaniel, brach or lym,
Or bobtail tike or trundle-tail,
Tom will make them weep and wail:
For, with throwing thus my head,
Dogs leap the hatch, and all are fled.
Do de, de, de. Sessa! Come, march to wakes and

fairs and market-towns. Poor Tom, thy horn is dry.
KING LEAR

Then let them anatomize Regan; see what breeds
about her heart. Is there any cause in nature that
makes these hard hearts?

To EDGAR

You, sir, I entertain for one of my hundred; only I
do not like the fashion of your garments: you will
say they are Persian attire: but let them be changed.
KENT

Now, good my lord, lie here and rest awhile.
KING LEAR

Make no noise, make no noise; draw the curtains:
so, so, so. We'll go to supper i' he morning. So, so, so.
Fool

And I'll go to bed at noon.

Re-enter GLOUCESTER

GLOUCESTER

Come hither, friend: where is the king my master?
KENT

Here, sir; but trouble him not, his wits are gone.
GLOUCESTER

Good friend, I prithee, take him in thy arms;
I have o'erheard a plot of death upon him:
There is a litter ready; lay him in 't,
And drive towards Dover, friend, where thou shalt meet
Both welcome and protection. Take up thy master:
If thou shouldst dally half an hour, his life,
With thine, and all that offer to defend him,
Stand in assured loss: take up, take up;
And follow me, that will to some provision

Give thee quick conduct.
KENT
    Oppressed nature sleeps:
    This rest might yet have balm'd thy broken senses,
    Which, if convenience will not allow,
    Stand in hard cure.

To the Fool

    Come, help to bear thy master;
    Thou must not stay behind.
GLOUCESTER
    Come, come, away.

Exeunt all but EDGAR

EDGAR
    When we our betters see bearing our woes,
    We scarcely think our miseries our foes.
    Who alone suffers suffers most i' the mind,
    Leaving free things and happy shows behind:
    But then the mind much sufferance doth o'er skip,
    When grief hath mates, and bearing fellowship.
    How light and portable my pain seems now,
    When that which makes me bend makes the king bow,
    He childed as I father'd! Tom, away!
    Mark the high noises; and thyself bewray,
    When false opinion, whose wrong thought defiles thee,
    In thy just proof, repeals and reconciles thee.
    What will hap more to-night, safe 'scape the king!
    Lurk, lurk.

Exit

SCENE VII.

Gloucester's castle.

Enter CORNWALL, REGAN, GONERIL, EDMUND, and Servants

CORNWALL

Post speedily to my lord your husband; show him
this letter: the army of France is landed. Seek
out the villain Gloucester.

Exeunt some of the Servants

REGAN

Hang him instantly.

GONERIL

Pluck out his eyes.

CORNWALL

Leave him to my displeasure. Edmund, keep you our
sister company: the revenges we are bound to take
upon your traitorous father are not fit for your
beholding. Advise the duke, where you are going, to
a most festinate preparation: we are bound to the
like. Our posts shall be swift and intelligent
betwixt us. Farewell, dear sister: farewell, my
lord of Gloucester.

Enter OSWALD

How now! where's the king?

OSWALD

My lord of Gloucester hath convey'd him hence:
Some five or six and thirty of his knights,
Hot questrists after him, met him at gate;
Who, with some other of the lords dependants,

Are gone with him towards Dover; where they boast
To have well-armed friends.

CORNWALL

Get horses for your mistress.

GONERIL

Farewell, sweet lord, and sister.

CORNWALL

Edmund, farewell.

Exeunt GONERIL, EDMUND, and OSWALD

Go seek the traitor Gloucester,
Pinion him like a thief, bring him before us.

Exeunt other Servants

Though well we may not pass upon his life
Without the form of justice, yet our power
Shall do a courtesy to our wrath, which men
May blame, but not control. Who's there? the traitor?

Enter GLOUCESTER, brought in by two or three

REGAN

Ingrateful fox! 'tis he.

CORNWALL

Bind fast his corky arms.

GLOUCESTER

What mean your graces? Good my friends, consider
You are my guests: do me no foul play, friends.

CORNWALL

Bind him, I say.

Servants bind him

REGAN

Hard, hard. O filthy traitor!

GLOUCESTER
Unmerciful lady as you are, I'm none.
CORNWALL
To this chair bind him. Villain, thou shalt find--

REGAN plucks his beard

GLOUCESTER
By the kind gods, 'tis most ignobly done
To pluck me by the beard.
REGAN
So white, and such a traitor!
GLOUCESTER
Naughty lady,
These hairs, which thou dost ravish from my chin,
Will quicken, and accuse thee: I am your host:
With robbers' hands my hospitable favours
You should not ruffle thus. What will you do?
CORNWALL
Come, sir, what letters had you late from France?
REGAN
Be simple answerer, for we know the truth.
CORNWALL
And what confederacy have you with the traitors
Late footed in the kingdom?
REGAN
To whose hands have you sent the lunatic king? Speak.
GLOUCESTER
I have a letter guessingly set down,
Which came from one that's of a neutral heart,
And not from one opposed.
CORNWALL
Cunning.
REGAN
And false.

CORNWALL
Where hast thou sent the king?
GLOUCESTER
To Dover.
REGAN
Wherefore to Dover? Wast thou not charged at peril--
CORNWALL
Wherefore to Dover? Let him first answer that.
GLOUCESTER
I am tied to the stake, and I must stand the course.
REGAN
Wherefore to Dover, sir?
GLOUCESTER
Because I would not see thy cruel nails
Pluck out his poor old eyes; nor thy fierce sister
In his anointed flesh stick boarish fangs.
The sea, with such a storm as his bare head
In hell-black night endured, would have buoy'd up,
And quench'd the stelled fires:
Yet, poor old heart, he holp the heavens to rain.
If wolves had at thy gate howl'd that stern time,
Thou shouldst have said 'Good porter, turn the key,'
All cruels else subscribed: but I shall see
The winged vengeance overtake such children.
CORNWALL
See't shalt thou never. Fellows, hold the chair.
Upon these eyes of thine I'll set my foot.
GLOUCESTER
He that will think to live till he be old,
Give me some help! O cruel! O you gods!
REGAN
One side will mock another; the other too.
CORNWALL
If you see vengeance,--

First Servant

Hold your hand, my lord:
I have served you ever since I was a child;
But better service have I never done you
Than now to bid you hold.

REGAN

How now, you dog!

First Servant

If you did wear a beard upon your chin,
I'd shake it on this quarrel. What do you mean?

CORNWALL

My villain!

They draw and fight

First Servant

Nay, then, come on, and take the chance of anger.

REGAN

Give me thy sword. A peasant stand up thus!

Takes a sword, and runs at him behind

First Servant

O, I am slain! My lord, you have one eye left
To see some mischief on him. O!

Dies

CORNWALL

Lest it see more, prevent it. Out, vile jelly!
Where is thy lustre now?

GLOUCESTER

All dark and comfortless. Where's my son Edmund?
Edmund, enkindle all the sparks of nature,
To quit this horrid act.

REGAN

Out, treacherous villain!

Thou call'st on him that hates thee: it was he
That made the overture of thy treasons to us;
Who is too good to pity thee.

GLOUCESTER

O my follies! then Edgar was abused.
Kind gods, forgive me that, and prosper him!

REGAN

Go thrust him out at gates, and let him smell
His way to Dover.

Exit one with GLOUCESTER

How is't, my lord? how look you?

CORNWALL

I have received a hurt: follow me, lady.
Turn out that eyeless villain; throw this slave
Upon the dunghill. Regan, I bleed apace:
Untimely comes this hurt: give me your arm.

Exit CORNWALL, led by REGAN

Second Servant

I'll never care what wickedness I do,
If this man come to good.

Third Servant

If she live long,
And in the end meet the old course of death,
Women will all turn monsters.

Second Servant

Let's follow the old earl, and get the Bedlam
To lead him where he would: his roguish madness
Allows itself to any thing.

Third Servant

Go thou: I'll fetch some flax and whites of eggs
To apply to his bleeding face. Now, heaven help him!

Exeunt severally

ACT IV

SCENE I.

The heath.

Enter EDGAR

EDGAR

    Yet better thus, and known to be contemn'd,
    Than still contemn'd and flatter'd. To be worst,
    The lowest and most dejected thing of fortune,
    Stands still in esperance, lives not in fear:
    The lamentable change is from the best;
    The worst returns to laughter. Welcome, then,
    Thou unsubstantial air that I embrace!
    The wretch that thou hast blown unto the worst
    Owes nothing to thy blasts. But who comes here?

Enter GLOUCESTER, led by an Old Man

    My father, poorly led? World, world, O world!
    But that thy strange mutations make us hate thee,
    Lie would not yield to age.

Old Man

    O, my good lord, I have been your tenant, and
    your father's tenant, these fourscore years.

GLOUCESTER

    Away, get thee away; good friend, be gone:
    Thy comforts can do me no good at all;
    Thee they may hurt.

Old Man

    Alack, sir, you cannot see your way.

GLOUCESTER

    I have no way, and therefore want no eyes;

I stumbled when I saw: full oft 'tis seen,
Our means secure us, and our mere defects
Prove our commodities. O dear son Edgar,
The food of thy abused father's wrath!
Might I but live to see thee in my touch,
I'ld say I had eyes again!

Old Man

How now! Who's there?

EDGAR

[Aside] O gods! Who is't can say 'I am at
the worst'?
I am worse than e'er I was.

Old Man

'Tis poor mad Tom.

EDGAR

[Aside] And worse I may be yet: the worst is not
So long as we can say 'This is the worst.'

Old Man

Fellow, where goest?

GLOUCESTER

Is it a beggar-man?

Old Man

Madman and beggar too.

GLOUCESTER

He has some reason, else he could not beg.
I' the last night's storm I such a fellow saw;
Which made me think a man a worm: my son
Came then into my mind; and yet my mind
Was then scarce friends with him: I have heard
more since.
As flies to wanton boys, are we to the gods.
They kill us for their sport.

EDGAR

[Aside]   How should this be?

Bad is the trade that must play fool to sorrow,
Angering itself and others.--Bless thee, master!
GLOUCESTER
Is that the naked fellow?
Old Man
Ay, my lord.
GLOUCESTER
Then, prithee, get thee gone: if, for my sake,
Thou wilt o'ertake us, hence a mile or twain,
I' the way toward Dover, do it for ancient love;
And bring some covering for this naked soul,
Who I'll entreat to lead me.
Old Man
Alack, sir, he is mad.
GLOUCESTER
'Tis the times' plague, when madmen lead the blind.
Do as I bid thee, or rather do thy pleasure;
Above the rest, be gone.
Old Man
I'll bring him the best 'parel that I have,
Come on't what will.

Exit

GLOUCESTER
Sirrah, naked fellow,--
EDGAR
Poor Tom's a-cold.

Aside

I cannot daub it further.
GLOUCESTER
Come hither, fellow.
EDGAR

[Aside] And yet I must.--Bless thy sweet eyes, they
bleed.
GLOUCESTER
Know'st thou the way to Dover?
EDGAR
Both stile and gate, horse-way and foot-path. Poor
Tom hath been scared out of his good wits: bless
thee, good man's son, from the foul fiend! five
fiends have been in poor Tom at once; of lust, as
Obidicut; Hobbididence, prince of dumbness; Mahu, of
stealing; Modo, of murder; Flibbertigibbet, of
mopping and mowing, who since possesses
chambermaids
and waiting-women. So, bless thee, master!
GLOUCESTER
Here, take this purse, thou whom the heavens' plagues
Have humbled to all strokes: that I am wretched
Makes thee the happier: heavens, deal so still!
Let the superfluous and lust-dieted man,
That slaves your ordinance, that will not see
Because he doth not feel, feel your power quickly;
So distribution should undo excess,
And each man have enough. Dost thou know Dover?
EDGAR
Ay, master.
GLOUCESTER
There is a cliff, whose high and bending head
Looks fearfully in the confined deep:
Bring me but to the very brim of it,
And I'll repair the misery thou dost bear
With something rich about me: from that place
I shall no leading need.
EDGAR
Give me thy arm:

107

Poor Tom shall lead thee.

Exeunt

SCENE II.

Before ALBANY's palace.

Enter GONERIL and EDMUND

GONERIL

Welcome, my lord: I marvel our mild husband
Not met us on the way.

Enter OSWALD

Now, where's your master'?

OSWALD

Madam, within; but never man so changed.
I told him of the army that was landed;
He smiled at it: I told him you were coming:
His answer was 'The worse:' of Gloucester's treachery,
And of the loyal service of his son,
When I inform'd him, then he call'd me sot,
And told me I had turn'd the wrong side out:
What most he should dislike seems pleasant to him;
What like, offensive.

GONERIL

[To EDMUND] Then shall you go no further.
It is the cowish terror of his spirit,
That dares not undertake: he'll not feel wrongs
Which tie him to an answer. Our wishes on the way
May prove effects. Back, Edmund, to my brother;
Hasten his musters and conduct his powers:
I must change arms at home, and give the distaff
Into my husband's hands. This trusty servant

Shall pass between us: ere long you are like to hear,
If you dare venture in your own behalf,
A mistress's command. Wear this; spare speech;

Giving a favour

Decline your head: this kiss, if it durst speak,
Would stretch thy spirits up into the air:
Conceive, and fare thee well.
EDMUND
Yours in the ranks of death.
GONERIL
My most dear Gloucester!

Exit EDMUND

O, the difference of man and man!
To thee a woman's services are due:
My fool usurps my body.
OSWALD
Madam, here comes my lord.

Exit

Enter ALBANY

GONERIL
I have been worth the whistle.
ALBANY
O Goneril!
You are not worth the dust which the rude wind
Blows in your face. I fear your disposition:
That nature, which contemns its origin,
Cannot be border'd certain in itself;
She that herself will sliver and disbranch
From her material sap, perforce must wither

And come to deadly use.

GONERIL

No more; the text is foolish.

ALBANY

Wisdom and goodness to the vile seem vile:
Filths savour but themselves. What have you done?
Tigers, not daughters, what have you perform'd?
A father, and a gracious aged man,
Whose reverence even the head-lugg'd bear would lick,
Most barbarous, most degenerate! have you madded.
Could my good brother suffer you to do it?
A man, a prince, by him so benefited!
If that the heavens do not their visible spirits
Send quickly down to tame these vile offences,
It will come,
Humanity must perforce prey on itself,
Like monsters of the deep.

GONERIL

Milk-liver'd man!
That bear'st a cheek for blows, a head for wrongs;
Who hast not in thy brows an eye discerning
Thine honour from thy suffering; that not know'st
Fools do those villains pity who are punish'd
Ere they have done their mischief. Where's thy drum?
France spreads his banners in our noiseless land;
With plumed helm thy slayer begins threats;
Whiles thou, a moral fool, sit'st still, and criest
'Alack, why does he so?'

ALBANY

See thyself, devil!
Proper deformity seems not in the fiend
So horrid as in woman.

GONERIL

O vain fool!

ALBANY

Thou changed and self-cover'd thing, for shame,
Be-monster not thy feature. Were't my fitness
To let these hands obey my blood,
They are apt enough to dislocate and tear
Thy flesh and bones: howe'er thou art a fiend,
A woman's shape doth shield thee.

GONERIL

Marry, your manhood now--

Enter a Messenger

ALBANY

What news?

Messenger

O, my good lord, the Duke of Cornwall's dead:
Slain by his servant, going to put out
The other eye of Gloucester.

ALBANY

Gloucester's eye!

Messenger

A servant that he bred, thrill'd with remorse,
Opposed against the act, bending his sword
To his great master; who, thereat enraged,
Flew on him, and amongst them fell'd him dead;
But not without that harmful stroke, which since
Hath pluck'd him after.

ALBANY

This shows you are above,
You justicers, that these our nether crimes
So speedily can venge! But, O poor Gloucester!
Lost he his other eye?

Messenger

Both, both, my lord.
This letter, madam, craves a speedy answer;

'Tis from your sister.
GONERIL
   [Aside] One way I like this well;
   But being widow, and my Gloucester with her,
   May all the building in my fancy pluck
   Upon my hateful life: another way,
   The news is not so tart.--I'll read, and answer.

Exit

ALBANY
   Where was his son when they did take his eyes?
Messenger
   Come with my lady hither.
ALBANY
   He is not here.
Messenger
   No, my good lord; I met him back again.
ALBANY
   Knows he the wickedness?
Messenger
   Ay, my good lord; 'twas he inform'd against him;
   And quit the house on purpose, that their punishment
   Might have the freer course.
ALBANY
   Gloucester, I live
   To thank thee for the love thou show'dst the king,
   And to revenge thine eyes. Come hither, friend:
   Tell me what more thou know'st.

Exeunt

SCENE III.

The French camp near Dover.

Enter KENT and a Gentleman

KENT

Why the King of France is so suddenly gone back
know you the reason?

Gentleman

Something he left imperfect in the
state, which since his coming forth is thought
of; which imports to the kingdom so much
fear and danger, that his personal return was
most required and necessary.

KENT

Who hath he left behind him general?

Gentleman

The Marshal of France, Monsieur La Far.

KENT

Did your letters pierce the queen to any
demonstration of grief?

Gentleman

Ay, sir; she took them, read them in my presence;
And now and then an ample tear trill'd down
Her delicate cheek: it seem'd she was a queen
Over her passion; who, most rebel-like,
Sought to be king o'er her.

KENT

O, then it moved her.

Gentleman

Not to a rage: patience and sorrow strove
Who should express her goodliest. You have seen
Sunshine and rain at once: her smiles and tears
Were like a better way: those happy smilets,
That play'd on her ripe lip, seem'd not to know

What guests were in her eyes; which parted thence,
As pearls from diamonds dropp'd. In brief,
Sorrow would be a rarity most beloved,
If all could so become it.

KENT

Made she no verbal question?

Gentleman

'Faith, once or twice she heaved the name of 'father'
Pantingly forth, as if it press'd her heart:
Cried 'Sisters! sisters! Shame of ladies! sisters!
Kent! father! sisters! What, i' the storm? i' the night?
Let pity not be believed!' There she shook
The holy water from her heavenly eyes,
And clamour moisten'd: then away she started
To deal with grief alone.

KENT

It is the stars,
The stars above us, govern our conditions;
Else one self mate and mate could not beget
Such different issues. You spoke not with her since?

Gentleman

No.

KENT

Was this before the king return'd?

Gentleman

No, since.

KENT

Well, sir, the poor distressed Lear's i' the town;
Who sometime, in his better tune, remembers
What we are come about, and by no means
Will yield to see his daughter.

Gentleman

Why, good sir?

KENT

A sovereign shame so elbows him: his own unkindness,
That stripp'd her from his benediction, turn'd her
To foreign casualties, gave her dear rights
To his dog-hearted daughters, these things sting
His mind so venomously, that burning shame
Detains him from Cordelia.

Gentleman

Alack, poor gentleman!

KENT

Of Albany's and Cornwall's powers you heard not?

Gentleman

'Tis so, they are afoot.

KENT

Well, sir, I'll bring you to our master Lear,
And leave you to attend him: some dear cause
Will in concealment wrap me up awhile;
When I am known aright, you shall not grieve
Lending me this acquaintance. I pray you, go
Along with me.

Exeunt

SCENE IV.

The same. A tent.

Enter, with drum and colours, CORDELIA, Doctor, and Soldiers

CORDELIA

Alack, 'tis he: why, he was met even now
As mad as the vex'd sea; singing aloud;
Crown'd with rank fumiter and furrow-weeds,
With bur-docks, hemlock, nettles, cuckoo-flowers,
Darnel, and all the idle weeds that grow
In our sustaining corn. A century send forth;

115

Search every acre in the high-grown field,
And bring him to our eye.

Exit an Officer

What can man's wisdom
In the restoring his bereaved sense?
He that helps him take all my outward worth.
Doctor
There is means, madam:
Our foster-nurse of nature is repose,
The which he lacks; that to provoke in him,
Are many simples operative, whose power
Will close the eye of anguish.
CORDELIA
All blest secrets,
All you unpublish'd virtues of the earth,
Spring with my tears! be aidant and remediate
In the good man's distress! Seek, seek for him;
Lest his ungovern'd rage dissolve the life
That wants the means to lead it.

Enter a Messenger

Messenger
News, madam;
The British powers are marching hitherward.
CORDELIA
'Tis known before; our preparation stands
In expectation of them. O dear father,
It is thy business that I go about;
Therefore great France
My mourning and important tears hath pitied.
No blown ambition doth our arms incite,
But love, dear love, and our aged father's right:

116

Soon may I hear and see him!

Exeunt

SCENE V.

Gloucester's castle.

Enter REGAN and OSWALD

REGAN

But are my brother's powers set forth?

OSWALD

Ay, madam.

REGAN

Himself in person there?

OSWALD

Madam, with much ado:

Your sister is the better soldier.

REGAN

Lord Edmund spake not with your lord at home?

OSWALD

No, madam.

REGAN

What might import my sister's letter to him?

OSWALD

I know not, lady.

REGAN

'Faith, he is posted hence on serious matter.

It was great ignorance, Gloucester's eyes being out,

To let him live: where he arrives he moves

All hearts against us: Edmund, I think, is gone,

In pity of his misery, to dispatch

His nighted life: moreover, to descry

The strength o' the enemy.

OSWALD

I must needs after him, madam, with my letter.

REGAN

Our troops set forth to-morrow: stay with us;
The ways are dangerous.

OSWALD

I may not, madam:
My lady charged my duty in this business.

REGAN

Why should she write to Edmund? Might not you
Transport her purposes by word? Belike,
Something--I know not what: I'll love thee much,
Let me unseal the letter.

OSWALD

Madam, I had rather--

REGAN

I know your lady does not love her husband;
I am sure of that: and at her late being here
She gave strange oeillades and most speaking looks
To noble Edmund. I know you are of her bosom.

OSWALD

I, madam?

REGAN

I speak in understanding; you are; I know't:
Therefore I do advise you, take this note:
My lord is dead; Edmund and I have talk'd;
And more convenient is he for my hand
Than for your lady's: you may gather more.
If you do find him, pray you, give him this;
And when your mistress hears thus much from you,
I pray, desire her call her wisdom to her.
So, fare you well.
If you do chance to hear of that blind traitor,
Preferment falls on him that cuts him off.

OSWALD

Would I could meet him, madam! I should show
What party I do follow.
REGAN
　　Fare thee well.

Exeunt

SCENE VI.

Fields near Dover.

Enter GLOUCESTER, and EDGAR dressed like a peasant

GLOUCESTER
　　When shall we come to the top of that same hill?
EDGAR
　　You do climb up it now: look, how we labour.
GLOUCESTER
　　Methinks the ground is even.
EDGAR
　　Horrible steep.
　　Hark, do you hear the sea?
GLOUCESTER
　　No, truly.
EDGAR
　　Why, then, your other senses grow imperfect
　　By your eyes' anguish.
GLOUCESTER
　　So may it be, indeed:
　　Methinks thy voice is alter'd; and thou speak'st
　　In better phrase and matter than thou didst.
EDGAR
　　You're much deceived: in nothing am I changed
　　But in my garments.
GLOUCESTER
　　Methinks you're better spoken.

119

EDGAR

    Come on, sir; here's the place: stand still. How fearful
    And dizzy 'tis, to cast one's eyes so low!
    The crows and choughs that wing the midway air
    Show scarce so gross as beetles: half way down
    Hangs one that gathers samphire, dreadful trade!
    Methinks he seems no bigger than his head:
    The fishermen, that walk upon the beach,
    Appear like mice; and yond tall anchoring bark,
    Diminish'd to her cock; her cock, a buoy
    Almost too small for sight: the murmuring surge,
    That on the unnumber'd idle pebbles chafes,
    Cannot be heard so high. I'll look no more;
    Lest my brain turn, and the deficient sight
    Topple down headlong.

GLOUCESTER

    Set me where you stand.

EDGAR

    Give me your hand: you are now within a foot
    Of the extreme verge: for all beneath the moon
    Would I not leap upright.

GLOUCESTER

    Let go my hand.
    Here, friend, 's another purse; in it a jewel
    Well worth a poor man's taking: fairies and gods
    Prosper it with thee! Go thou farther off;
    Bid me farewell, and let me hear thee going.

EDGAR

    Now fare you well, good sir.

GLOUCESTER

    With all my heart.

EDGAR

    Why I do trifle thus with his despair
    Is done to cure it.

GLOUCESTER

[Kneeling] O you mighty gods!
This world I do renounce, and, in your sights,
Shake patiently my great affliction off:
If I could bear it longer, and not fall
To quarrel with your great opposeless wills,
My snuff and loathed part of nature should
Burn itself out. If Edgar live, O, bless him!
Now, fellow, fare thee well.

He falls forward

EDGAR

Gone, sir: farewell.
And yet I know not how conceit may rob
The treasury of life, when life itself
Yields to the theft: had he been where he thought,
By this, had thought been past. Alive or dead?
Ho, you sir! friend! Hear you, sir! speak!
Thus might he pass indeed: yet he revives.
What are you, sir?

GLOUCESTER

Away, and let me die.

EDGAR

Hadst thou been aught but gossamer, feathers, air,
So many fathom down precipitating,
Thou'dst shiver'd like an egg: but thou dost breathe;
Hast heavy substance; bleed'st not; speak'st; art sound.
Ten masts at each make not the altitude
Which thou hast perpendicularly fell:
Thy life's a miracle. Speak yet again.

GLOUCESTER

But have I fall'n, or no?

EDGAR

From the dread summit of this chalky bourn.

Look up a-height; the shrill-gorged lark so far
Cannot be seen or heard: do but look up.

GLOUCESTER

Alack, I have no eyes.
Is wretchedness deprived that benefit,
To end itself by death? 'Twas yet some comfort,
When misery could beguile the tyrant's rage,
And frustrate his proud will.

EDGAR

Give me your arm:
Up: so. How is 't? Feel you your legs? You stand.

GLOUCESTER

Too well, too well.

EDGAR

This is above all strangeness.
Upon the crown o' the cliff, what thing was that
Which parted from you?

GLOUCESTER

A poor unfortunate beggar.

EDGAR

As I stood here below, methought his eyes
Were two full moons; he had a thousand noses,
Horns whelk'd and waved like the enridged sea:
It was some fiend; therefore, thou happy father,
Think that the clearest gods, who make them honours
Of men's impossibilities, have preserved thee.

GLOUCESTER

I do remember now: henceforth I'll bear
Affliction till it do cry out itself
'Enough, enough,' and die. That thing you speak of,
I took it for a man; often 'twould say
'The fiend, the fiend:' he led me to that place.

EDGAR

Bear free and patient thoughts. But who comes here?

Enter KING LEAR, fantastically dressed with wild flowers

The safer sense will ne'er accommodate
His master thus.

KING LEAR

No, they cannot touch me for coining; I am the
king himself.

EDGAR

O thou side-piercing sight!

KING LEAR

Nature's above art in that respect. There's your
press-money. That fellow handles his bow like a
crow-keeper: draw me a clothier's yard. Look,
look, a mouse! Peace, peace; this piece of toasted
cheese will do 't. There's my gauntlet; I'll prove
it on a giant. Bring up the brown bills. O, well
flown, bird! i' the clout, i' the clout: hewgh!
Give the word.

EDGAR

Sweet marjoram.

KING LEAR

Pass.

GLOUCESTER

I know that voice.

KING LEAR

Ha! Goneril, with a white beard! They flattered
me like a dog; and told me I had white hairs in my
beard ere the black ones were there. To say 'ay'
and 'no' to every thing that I said!--'Ay' and 'no'
too was no good divinity. When the rain came to
wet me once, and the wind to make me chatter; when
the thunder would not peace at my bidding; there I
found 'em, there I smelt 'em out. Go to, they are
not men o' their words: they told me I was every

thing; 'tis a lie, I am not ague-proof.

GLOUCESTER

The trick of that voice I do well remember:
Is 't not the king?

KING LEAR

Ay, every inch a king:
When I do stare, see how the subject quakes.
I pardon that man's life. What was thy cause? Adultery?
Thou shalt not die: die for adultery! No:
The wren goes to 't, and the small gilded fly
Does lecher in my sight.
Let copulation thrive; for Gloucester's bastard son
Was kinder to his father than my daughters
Got 'tween the lawful sheets.
To 't, luxury, pell-mell! for I lack soldiers.
Behold yond simpering dame,
Whose face between her forks presages snow;
That minces virtue, and does shake the head
To hear of pleasure's name;
The fitchew, nor the soiled horse, goes to 't
With a more riotous appetite.
Down from the waist they are Centaurs,
Though women all above:
But to the girdle do the gods inherit,
Beneath is all the fiends';
There's hell, there's darkness, there's the
sulphurous pit,
Burning, scalding, stench, consumption; fie,
fie, fie! pah, pah! Give me an ounce of civet,
good apothecary, to sweeten my imagination:
there's money for thee.

GLOUCESTER

O, let me kiss that hand!

KING LEAR

Let me wipe it first; it smells of mortality.

GLOUCESTER

O ruin'd piece of nature! This great world
Shall so wear out to nought. Dost thou know me?

KING LEAR

I remember thine eyes well enough. Dost thou squiny
at me? No, do thy worst, blind Cupid! I'll not
love. Read thou this challenge; mark but the
penning of it.

GLOUCESTER

Were all the letters suns, I could not see one.

EDGAR

I would not take this from report; it is,
And my heart breaks at it.

KING LEAR

Read.

GLOUCESTER

What, with the case of eyes?

KING LEAR

O, ho, are you there with me? No eyes in your
head, nor no money in your purse? Your eyes are in
a heavy case, your purse in a light; yet you see how
this world goes.

GLOUCESTER

I see it feelingly.

KING LEAR

What, art mad? A man may see how this world goes
with no eyes. Look with thine ears: see how yond
justice rails upon yond simple thief. Hark, in
thine ear: change places; and, handy-dandy, which
is the justice, which is the thief? Thou hast seen
a farmer's dog bark at a beggar?

GLOUCESTER

Ay, sir.

KING LEAR

And the creature run from the cur? There thou
mightst behold the great image of authority: a
dog's obeyed in office.
Thou rascal beadle, hold thy bloody hand!
Why dost thou lash that whore? Strip thine own back;
Thou hotly lust'st to use her in that kind
For which thou whipp'st her. The usurer hangs the
cozener.
Through tatter'd clothes small vices do appear;
Robes and furr'd gowns hide all. Plate sin with gold,
And the strong lance of justice hurtless breaks:
Arm it in rags, a pigmy's straw does pierce it.
None does offend, none, I say, none; I'll able 'em:
Take that of me, my friend, who have the power
To seal the accuser's lips. Get thee glass eyes;
And like a scurvy politician, seem
To see the things thou dost not. Now, now, now, now:
Pull off my boots: harder, harder: so.

EDGAR

O, matter and impertinency mix'd! Reason in madness!

KING LEAR

If thou wilt weep my fortunes, take my eyes.
I know thee well enough; thy name is Gloucester:
Thou must be patient; we came crying hither:
Thou know'st, the first time that we smell the air,
We wawl and cry. I will preach to thee: mark.

GLOUCESTER

Alack, alack the day!

KING LEAR

When we are born, we cry that we are come
To this great stage of fools: this a good block;
It were a delicate stratagem, to shoe
A troop of horse with felt: I'll put 't in proof;

126

And when I have stol'n upon these sons-in-law,
Then, kill, kill, kill, kill, kill, kill!

Enter a Gentleman, with Attendants

Gentleman

O, here he is: lay hand upon him. Sir,
Your most dear daughter--
KING LEAR

No rescue? What, a prisoner? I am even
The natural fool of fortune. Use me well;
You shall have ransom. Let me have surgeons;
I am cut to the brains.
Gentleman

You shall have any thing.
KING LEAR

No seconds? all myself?
Why, this would make a man a man of salt,
To use his eyes for garden water-pots,
Ay, and laying autumn's dust.
Gentleman

Good sir,--
KING LEAR

I will die bravely, like a bridegroom. What!
I will be jovial: come, come; I am a king,
My masters, know you that.
Gentleman

You are a royal one, and we obey you.
KING LEAR

Then there's life in't. Nay, if you get it, you
shall get it with running. Sa, sa, sa, sa.

Exit running; Attendants follow

Gentleman

A sight most pitiful in the meanest wretch,
Past speaking of in a king! Thou hast one daughter,
Who redeems nature from the general curse
Which twain have brought her to.
EDGAR
Hail, gentle sir.
Gentleman
Sir, speed you: what's your will?
EDGAR
Do you hear aught, sir, of a battle toward?
Gentleman
Most sure and vulgar: every one hears that,
Which can distinguish sound.
EDGAR
But, by your favour,
How near's the other army?
Gentleman
Near and on speedy foot; the main descry
Stands on the hourly thought.
EDGAR
I thank you, sir: that's all.
Gentleman
Though that the queen on special cause is here,
Her army is moved on.
EDGAR
I thank you, sir.

Exit Gentleman

GLOUCESTER
You ever-gentle gods, take my breath from me:
Let not my worser spirit tempt me again
To die before you please!
EDGAR
Well pray you, father.

GLOUCESTER
Now, good sir, what are you?
EDGAR
A most poor man, made tame to fortune's blows;
Who, by the art of known and feeling sorrows,
Am pregnant to good pity. Give me your hand,
I'll lead you to some biding.
GLOUCESTER
Hearty thanks:
The bounty and the benison of heaven
To boot, and boot!

Enter OSWALD

OSWALD
A proclaim'd prize! Most happy!
That eyeless head of thine was first framed flesh
To raise my fortunes. Thou old unhappy traitor,
Briefly thyself remember: the sword is out
That must destroy thee.
GLOUCESTER
Now let thy friendly hand
Put strength enough to't.

EDGAR interposes

OSWALD
Wherefore, bold peasant,
Darest thou support a publish'd traitor? Hence;
Lest that the infection of his fortune take
Like hold on thee. Let go his arm.
EDGAR
Ch'ill not let go, zir, without vurther 'casion.
OSWALD
Let go, slave, or thou diest!

EDGAR

Good gentleman, go your gait, and let poor volk
pass. An chud ha' bin zwaggered out of my life,
'twould not ha' bin zo long as 'tis by a vortnight.
Nay, come not near th' old man; keep out, che vor
ye, or ise try whether your costard or my ballow be
the harder: ch'ill be plain with you.

OSWALD

Out, dunghill!

EDGAR

Ch'ill pick your teeth, zir: come; no matter vor
your foins.

They fight, and EDGAR knocks him down

OSWALD

Slave, thou hast slain me: villain, take my purse:
If ever thou wilt thrive, bury my body;
And give the letters which thou find'st about me
To Edmund earl of Gloucester; seek him out
Upon the British party: O, untimely death!

Dies

EDGAR

I know thee well: a serviceable villain;
As duteous to the vices of thy mistress
As badness would desire.

GLOUCESTER

What, is he dead?

EDGAR

Sit you down, father; rest you
Let's see these pockets: the letters that he speaks of
May be my friends. He's dead; I am only sorry
He had no other death's-man. Let us see:

Leave, gentle wax; and, manners, blame us not:
To know our enemies' minds, we'ld rip their hearts;
Their papers, is more lawful.

Reads

'Let our reciprocal vows be remembered. You have
many opportunities to cut him off: if your will
want not, time and place will be fruitfully offered.
There is nothing done, if he return the conqueror:
then am I the prisoner, and his bed my goal; from
the loathed warmth whereof deliver me, and supply
the place for your labour.
'Your--wife, so I would say--
Affectionate servant,
        Goneril.'
O undistinguish'd space of woman's will!
A plot upon her virtuous husband's life;
And the exchange my brother! Here, in the sands,
Thee I'll rake up, the post unsanctified
Of murderous lechers: and in the mature time
With this ungracious paper strike the sight
Of the death practised duke: for him 'tis well
That of thy death and business I can tell.
GLOUCESTER
The king is mad: how stiff is my vile sense,
That I stand up, and have ingenious feeling
Of my huge sorrows! Better I were distract:
So should my thoughts be sever'd from my griefs,
And woes by wrong imaginations lose
The knowledge of themselves.
EDGAR
Give me your hand:

Drum afar off

131

Far off, methinks, I hear the beaten drum:
Come, father, I'll bestow you with a friend.

Exeunt

SCENE VII.

A tent in the French camp. LEAR on a bed asleep,

soft music playing; Gentleman, and others attending.

Enter CORDELIA, KENT, and Doctor

CORDELIA

O thou good Kent, how shall I live and work,
To match thy goodness? My life will be too short,
And every measure fail me.

KENT

To be acknowledged, madam, is o'erpaid.
All my reports go with the modest truth;
Nor more nor clipp'd, but so.

CORDELIA

Be better suited:
These weeds are memories of those worser hours:
I prithee, put them off.

KENT

Pardon me, dear madam;
Yet to be known shortens my made intent:
My boon I make it, that you know me not
Till time and I think meet.

CORDELIA

Then be't so, my good lord.

To the Doctor

How does the king?

Doctor

Madam, sleeps still.

CORDELIA

O you kind gods,
Cure this great breach in his abused nature!
The untuned and jarring senses, O, wind up
Of this child-changed father!

Doctor

So please your majesty
That we may wake the king: he hath slept long.

CORDELIA

Be govern'd by your knowledge, and proceed
I' the sway of your own will. Is he array'd?

Gentleman

Ay, madam; in the heaviness of his sleep
We put fresh garments on him.

Doctor

Be by, good madam, when we do awake him;
I doubt not of his temperance.

CORDELIA

Very well.

Doctor

Please you, draw near. Louder the music there!

CORDELIA

O my dear father! Restoration hang
Thy medicine on my lips; and let this kiss
Repair those violent harms that my two sisters
Have in thy reverence made!

KENT

Kind and dear princess!

CORDELIA

Had you not been their father, these white flakes
Had challenged pity of them. Was this a face
To be opposed against the warring winds?
To stand against the deep dread-bolted thunder?

In the most terrible and nimble stroke
Of quick, cross lightning? to watch--poor perdu!--
With this thin helm? Mine enemy's dog,
Though he had bit me, should have stood that night
Against my fire; and wast thou fain, poor father,
To hovel thee with swine, and rogues forlorn,
In short and musty straw? Alack, alack!
'Tis wonder that thy life and wits at once
Had not concluded all. He wakes; speak to him.
Doctor
Madam, do you; 'tis fittest.
CORDELIA
How does my royal lord? How fares your majesty?
KING LEAR
You do me wrong to take me out o' the grave:
Thou art a soul in bliss; but I am bound
Upon a wheel of fire, that mine own tears
Do scald like moulten lead.
CORDELIA
Sir, do you know me?
KING LEAR
You are a spirit, I know: when did you die?
CORDELIA
Still, still, far wide!
Doctor
He's scarce awake: let him alone awhile.
KING LEAR
Where have I been? Where am I? Fair daylight?
I am mightily abused. I should e'en die with pity,
To see another thus. I know not what to say.
I will not swear these are my hands: let's see;
I feel this pin prick. Would I were assured
Of my condition!
CORDELIA

O, look upon me, sir,
And hold your hands in benediction o'er me:
No, sir, you must not kneel.

KING LEAR

Pray, do not mock me:
I am a very foolish fond old man,
Fourscore and upward, not an hour more nor less;
And, to deal plainly,
I fear I am not in my perfect mind.
Methinks I should know you, and know this man;
Yet I am doubtful for I am mainly ignorant
What place this is; and all the skill I have
Remembers not these garments; nor I know not
Where I did lodge last night. Do not laugh at me;
For, as I am a man, I think this lady
To be my child Cordelia.

CORDELIA

And so I am, I am.

KING LEAR

Be your tears wet? yes, 'faith. I pray, weep not:
If you have poison for me, I will drink it.
I know you do not love me; for your sisters
Have, as I do remember, done me wrong:
You have some cause, they have not.

CORDELIA

No cause, no cause.

KING LEAR

Am I in France?

KENT

In your own kingdom, sir.

KING LEAR

Do not abuse me.

Doctor

Be comforted, good madam: the great rage,

You see, is kill'd in him: and yet it is danger
To make him even o'er the time he has lost.
Desire him to go in; trouble him no more
Till further settling.

CORDELIA

Will't please your highness walk?

KING LEAR

You must bear with me:
Pray you now, forget and forgive: I am old and foolish.

Exeunt all but KENT and Gentleman

Gentleman

Holds it true, sir, that the Duke of Cornwall was so
slain?

KENT

Most certain, sir.

Gentleman

Who is conductor of his people?

KENT

As 'tis said, the bastard son of Gloucester.

Gentleman

They say Edgar, his banished son, is with the Earl
of Kent in Germany.

KENT

Report is changeable. 'Tis time to look about; the
powers of the kingdom approach apace.

Gentleman

The arbitrement is like to be bloody. Fare you
well, sir.

Exit

KENT

My point and period will be throughly wrought,
Or well or ill, as this day's battle's fought.

Exit

ACT V

SCENE I.

The British camp, near Dover.

Enter, with drum and colours, EDMUND, REGAN, Gentlemen, and Soldiers.

EDMUND

Know of the duke if his last purpose hold,
Or whether since he is advised by aught
To change the course: he's full of alteration
And self-reproving: bring his constant pleasure.

To a Gentleman, who goes out

REGAN

Our sister's man is certainly miscarried.

EDMUND

'Tis to be doubted, madam.

REGAN

Now, sweet lord,
You know the goodness I intend upon you:
Tell me--but truly--but then speak the truth,
Do you not love my sister?

EDMUND

In honour'd love.

REGAN

But have you never found my brother's way
To the forfended place?

EDMUND

That thought abuses you.

REGAN

I am doubtful that you have been conjunct

And bosom'd with her, as far as we call hers.

EDMUND

No, by mine honour, madam.

REGAN

I never shall endure her: dear my lord,
Be not familiar with her.

EDMUND

Fear me not:
She and the duke her husband!

*Enter, with drum and colours, ALBANY, GONERIL, and
Soldiers*

GONERIL

[Aside] I had rather lose the battle than that sister
Should loosen him and me.

ALBANY

Our very loving sister, well be-met.
Sir, this I hear; the king is come to his daughter,
With others whom the rigor of our state
Forced to cry out. Where I could not be honest,
I never yet was valiant: for this business,
It toucheth us, as France invades our land,
Not bolds the king, with others, whom, I fear,
Most just and heavy causes make oppose.

EDMUND

Sir, you speak nobly.

REGAN

Why is this reason'd?

GONERIL

Combine together 'gainst the enemy;
For these domestic and particular broils
Are not the question here.

ALBANY

Let's then determine

With the ancient of war on our proceedings.

EDMUND

I shall attend you presently at your tent.

REGAN

Sister, you'll go with us?

GONERIL

No.

REGAN

'Tis most convenient; pray you, go with us.

GONERIL

[Aside] O, ho, I know the riddle.--I will go.

As they are going out, enter EDGAR disguised

EDGAR

If e'er your grace had speech with man so poor,
Hear me one word.

ALBANY

I'll overtake you. Speak.

Exeunt all but ALBANY and EDGAR

EDGAR

Before you fight the battle, ope this letter.
If you have victory, let the trumpet sound
For him that brought it: wretched though I seem,
I can produce a champion that will prove
What is avouched there. If you miscarry,
Your business of the world hath so an end,
And machination ceases. Fortune love you.

ALBANY

Stay till I have read the letter.

EDGAR

I was forbid it.
When time shall serve, let but the herald cry,

And I'll appear again.

ALBANY

Why, fare thee well: I will o'erlook thy paper.

Exit EDGAR

Re-enter EDMUND

EDMUND

The enemy's in view; draw up your powers.
Here is the guess of their true strength and forces
By diligent discovery; but your haste
Is now urged on you.

ALBANY

We will greet the time.

Exit

EDMUND

To both these sisters have I sworn my love;
Each jealous of the other, as the stung
Are of the adder. Which of them shall I take?
Both? one? or neither? Neither can be enjoy'd,
If both remain alive: to take the widow
Exasperates, makes mad her sister Goneril;
And hardly shall I carry out my side,
Her husband being alive. Now then we'll use
His countenance for the battle; which being done,
Let her who would be rid of him devise
His speedy taking off. As for the mercy
Which he intends to Lear and to Cordelia,
The battle done, and they within our power,
Shall never see his pardon; for my state
Stands on me to defend, not to debate.

Exit

SCENE II.

A field between the two camps.

Alarum within. Enter, with drum and colours, KING LEAR,
CORDELIA, and Soldiers, over the stage; and exeunt

Enter EDGAR and GLOUCESTER

EDGAR
    Here, father, take the shadow of this tree
    For your good host; pray that the right may thrive:
    If ever I return to you again,
    I'll bring you comfort.
GLOUCESTER
    Grace go with you, sir!

Exit EDGAR

Alarum and retreat within. Re-enter EDGAR

EDGAR
    Away, old man; give me thy hand; away!
    King Lear hath lost, he and his daughter ta'en:
    Give me thy hand; come on.
GLOUCESTER
    No farther, sir; a man may rot even here.
EDGAR
    What, in ill thoughts again? Men must endure
    Their going hence, even as their coming hither;
    Ripeness is all: come on.
GLOUCESTER
    And that's true too.

Exeunt

SCENE III.

The British camp near Dover.

Enter, in conquest, with drum and colours, EDMUND, KING LEAR and CORDELIA, prisoners; Captain, Soldiers, & c

EDMUND
  Some officers take them away: good guard,
  Until their greater pleasures first be known
  That are to censure them.
CORDELIA
  We are not the first
  Who, with best meaning, have incurr'd the worst.
  For thee, oppressed king, am I cast down;
  Myself could else out-frown false fortune's frown.
  Shall we not see these daughters and these sisters?
KING LEAR
  No, no, no, no! Come, let's away to prison:
  We two alone will sing like birds i' the cage:
  When thou dost ask me blessing, I'll kneel down,
  And ask of thee forgiveness: so we'll live,
  And pray, and sing, and tell old tales, and laugh
  At gilded butterflies, and hear poor rogues
  Talk of court news; and we'll talk with them too,
  Who loses and who wins; who's in, who's out;
  And take upon's the mystery of things,
  As if we were God's spies: and we'll wear out,
  In a wall'd prison, packs and sects of great ones,
  That ebb and flow by the moon.
EDMUND
  Take them away.
KING LEAR
  Upon such sacrifices, my Cordelia,
  The gods themselves throw incense. Have I caught thee?
  He that parts us shall bring a brand from heaven,

And fire us hence like foxes. Wipe thine eyes;
The good-years shall devour them, flesh and fell,
Ere they shall make us weep: we'll see 'em starve
first. Come.

Exeunt KING LEAR and CORDELIA, guarded

EDMUND
Come hither, captain; hark.
Take thou this note;

Giving a paper

go follow them to prison:
One step I have advanced thee; if thou dost
As this instructs thee, thou dost make thy way
To noble fortunes: know thou this, that men
Are as the time is: to be tender-minded
Does not become a sword: thy great employment
Will not bear question; either say thou'lt do 't,
Or thrive by other means.
Captain
I'll do 't, my lord.
EDMUND
About it; and write happy when thou hast done.
Mark, I say, instantly; and carry it so
As I have set it down.
Captain
I cannot draw a cart, nor eat dried oats;
If it be man's work, I'll do 't.

Exit

*Flourish. Enter ALBANY, GONERIL, REGAN, another
Captain, and Soldiers*

ALBANY

    Sir, you have shown to-day your valiant strain,
    And fortune led you well: you have the captives
    That were the opposites of this day's strife:
    We do require them of you, so to use them
    As we shall find their merits and our safety
    May equally determine.

EDMUND

    Sir, I thought it fit
    To send the old and miserable king
    To some retention and appointed guard;
    Whose age has charms in it, whose title more,
    To pluck the common bosom on his side,
    An turn our impress'd lances in our eyes
    Which do command them. With him I sent the queen;
    My reason all the same; and they are ready
    To-morrow, or at further space, to appear
    Where you shall hold your session. At this time
    We sweat and bleed: the friend hath lost his friend;
    And the best quarrels, in the heat, are cursed
    By those that feel their sharpness:
    The question of Cordelia and her father
    Requires a fitter place.

ALBANY

    Sir, by your patience,
    I hold you but a subject of this war,
    Not as a brother.

REGAN

    That's as we list to grace him.
    Methinks our pleasure might have been demanded,
    Ere you had spoke so far. He led our powers;
    Bore the commission of my place and person;
    The which immediacy may well stand up,
    And call itself your brother.

GONERIL

    Not so hot:

    In his own grace he doth exalt himself,

    More than in your addition.

REGAN

    In my rights,

    By me invested, he compeers the best.

GONERIL

    That were the most, if he should husband you.

REGAN

    Jesters do oft prove prophets.

GONERIL

    Holla, holla!

    That eye that told you so look'd but a-squint.

REGAN

    Lady, I am not well; else I should answer

    From a full-flowing stomach. General,

    Take thou my soldiers, prisoners, patrimony;

    Dispose of them, of me; the walls are thine:

    Witness the world, that I create thee here

    My lord and master.

GONERIL

    Mean you to enjoy him?

ALBANY

    The let-alone lies not in your good will.

EDMUND

    Nor in thine, lord.

ALBANY

    Half-blooded fellow, yes.

REGAN

[To EDMUND] Let the drum strike, and prove my title thine.

ALBANY

    Stay yet; hear reason. Edmund, I arrest thee

On capital treason; and, in thine attaint,
This gilded serpent

Pointing to Goneril

For your claim, fair sister,
I bar it in the interest of my wife:
'Tis she is sub-contracted to this lord,
And I, her husband, contradict your bans.
If you will marry, make your loves to me,
My lady is bespoke.
GONERIL
An interlude!
ALBANY
Thou art arm'd, Gloucester: let the trumpet sound:
If none appear to prove upon thy head
Thy heinous, manifest, and many treasons,
There is my pledge;

Throwing down a glove

I'll prove it on thy heart,
Ere I taste bread, thou art in nothing less
Than I have here proclaim'd thee.
REGAN
Sick, O, sick!
GONERIL
[Aside] If not, I'll ne'er trust medicine.
EDMUND
There's my exchange:

Throwing down a glove

what in the world he is
That names me traitor, villain-like he lies:
Call by thy trumpet: he that dares approach,

On him, on you, who not? I will maintain
My truth and honour firmly.
ALBANY
A herald, ho!
EDMUND
A herald, ho, a herald!
ALBANY
Trust to thy single virtue; for thy soldiers,
All levied in my name, have in my name
Took their discharge.
REGAN
My sickness grows upon me.
ALBANY
She is not well; convey her to my tent.

Exit Regan, led

Enter a Herald

Come hither, herald,--Let the trumpet sound,
And read out this.
Captain
Sound, trumpet!

A trumpet sounds

Herald
[Reads] 'If any man of quality or degree within
the lists of the army will maintain upon Edmund,
supposed Earl of Gloucester, that he is a manifold
traitor, let him appear by the third sound of the
trumpet: he is bold in his defence.'
EDMUND
Sound!

First trumpet

Herald
    Again!

Second trumpet

Herald
    Again!

Third trumpet

Trumpet answers within

Enter EDGAR, at the third sound, armed, with a trumpet before him

ALBANY
    Ask him his purposes, why he appears
    Upon this call o' the trumpet.
Herald
    What are you?
    Your name, your quality? and why you answer
    This present summons?
EDGAR
    Know, my name is lost;
    By treason's tooth bare-gnawn and canker-bit:
    Yet am I noble as the adversary
    I come to cope.
ALBANY
    Which is that adversary?
EDGAR
    What's he that speaks for Edmund Earl of Gloucester?
EDMUND
    Himself: what say'st thou to him?
EDGAR

Draw thy sword,
That, if my speech offend a noble heart,
Thy arm may do thee justice: here is mine.
Behold, it is the privilege of mine honours,
My oath, and my profession: I protest,
Maugre thy strength, youth, place, and eminence,
Despite thy victor sword and fire-new fortune,
Thy valour and thy heart, thou art a traitor;
False to thy gods, thy brother, and thy father;
Conspirant 'gainst this high-illustrious prince;
And, from the extremest upward of thy head
To the descent and dust below thy foot,
A most toad-spotted traitor. Say thou 'No,'
This sword, this arm, and my best spirits, are bent
To prove upon thy heart, whereto I speak,
Thou liest.

EDMUND

In wisdom I should ask thy name;
But, since thy outside looks so fair and warlike,
And that thy tongue some say of breeding breathes,
What safe and nicely I might well delay
By rule of knighthood, I disdain and spurn:
Back do I toss these treasons to thy head;
With the hell-hated lie o'erwhelm thy heart;
Which, for they yet glance by and scarcely bruise,
This sword of mine shall give them instant way,
Where they shall rest for ever. Trumpets, speak!

Alarums. They fight. EDMUND falls

ALBANY

Save him, save him!

GONERIL

This is practise, Gloucester:
By the law of arms thou wast not bound to answer

149

An unknown opposite; thou art not vanquish'd,
But cozen'd and beguiled.

ALBANY

Shut your mouth, dame,
Or with this paper shall I stop it: Hold, sir:
Thou worse than any name, read thine own evil:
No tearing, lady: I perceive you know it.

Gives the letter to EDMUND

GONERIL

Say, if I do, the laws are mine, not thine:
Who can arraign me for't.

ALBANY

Most monstrous! oh!
Know'st thou this paper?

GONERIL

Ask me not what I know.

Exit

ALBANY

Go after her: she's desperate; govern her.

EDMUND

What you have charged me with, that have I done;
And more, much more; the time will bring it out:
'Tis past, and so am I. But what art thou
That hast this fortune on me? If thou'rt noble,
I do forgive thee.

EDGAR

Let's exchange charity.
I am no less in blood than thou art, Edmund;
If more, the more thou hast wrong'd me.
My name is Edgar, and thy father's son.
The gods are just, and of our pleasant vices

Make instruments to plague us:
The dark and vicious place where thee he got
Cost him his eyes.

EDMUND

Thou hast spoken right, 'tis true;
The wheel is come full circle: I am here.

ALBANY

Methought thy very gait did prophesy
A royal nobleness: I must embrace thee:
Let sorrow split my heart, if ever I
Did hate thee or thy father!

EDGAR

Worthy prince, I know't.

ALBANY

Where have you hid yourself?
How have you known the miseries of your father?

EDGAR

By nursing them, my lord. List a brief tale;
And when 'tis told, O, that my heart would burst!
The bloody proclamation to escape,
That follow'd me so near,--O, our lives' sweetness!
That we the pain of death would hourly die
Rather than die at once!--taught me to shift
Into a madman's rags; to assume a semblance
That very dogs disdain'd: and in this habit
Met I my father with his bleeding rings,
Their precious stones new lost: became his guide,
Led him, begg'd for him, saved him from despair;
Never,--O fault!--reveal'd myself unto him,
Until some half-hour past, when I was arm'd:
Not sure, though hoping, of this good success,
I ask'd his blessing, and from first to last
Told him my pilgrimage: but his flaw'd heart,
Alack, too weak the conflict to support!

'Twixt two extremes of passion, joy and grief,
Burst smilingly.

EDMUND

This speech of yours hath moved me,
And shall perchance do good: but speak you on;
You look as you had something more to say.

ALBANY

If there be more, more woeful, hold it in;
For I am almost ready to dissolve,
Hearing of this.

EDGAR

This would have seem'd a period
To such as love not sorrow; but another,
To amplify too much, would make much more,
And top extremity.
Whilst I was big in clamour came there in a man,
Who, having seen me in my worst estate,
Shunn'd my abhorr'd society; but then, finding
Who 'twas that so endured, with his strong arms
He fastened on my neck, and bellow'd out
As he'ld burst heaven; threw him on my father;
Told the most piteous tale of Lear and him
That ever ear received: which in recounting
His grief grew puissant and the strings of life
Began to crack: twice then the trumpets sounded,
And there I left him tranced.

ALBANY

But who was this?

EDGAR

Kent, sir, the banish'd Kent; who in disguise
Follow'd his enemy king, and did him service
Improper for a slave.

Enter a Gentleman, with a bloody knife

Gentleman
  Help, help, O, help!
EDGAR
  What kind of help?
ALBANY
  Speak, man.
EDGAR
  What means that bloody knife?
Gentleman
  'Tis hot, it smokes;
  It came even from the heart of--O, she's dead!
ALBANY
  Who dead? speak, man.
Gentleman
  Your lady, sir, your lady: and her sister
  By her is poisoned; she hath confess'd it.
EDMUND
  I was contracted to them both: all three
  Now marry in an instant.
EDGAR
  Here comes Kent.
ALBANY
  Produce their bodies, be they alive or dead:
  This judgment of the heavens, that makes us tremble,
  Touches us not with pity.

Exit Gentleman

Enter KENT

  O, is this he?
  The time will not allow the compliment
  Which very manners urges.
KENT

I am come
To bid my king and master aye good night:
Is he not here?

ALBANY

Great thing of us forgot!
Speak, Edmund, where's the king? and where's
Cordelia?
See'st thou this object, Kent?

The bodies of GONERIL and REGAN are brought in

KENT

Alack, why thus?

EDMUND

Yet Edmund was beloved:
The one the other poison'd for my sake,
And after slew herself.

ALBANY

Even so. Cover their faces.

EDMUND

I pant for life: some good I mean to do,
Despite of mine own nature. Quickly send,
Be brief in it, to the castle; for my writ
Is on the life of Lear and on Cordelia:
Nay, send in time.

ALBANY

Run, run, O, run!

EDGAR

To who, my lord? Who hath the office? send
Thy token of reprieve.

EDMUND

Well thought on: take my sword,
Give it the captain.

ALBANY

Haste thee, for thy life.

Exit EDGAR

EDMUND

He hath commission from thy wife and me
To hang Cordelia in the prison, and
To lay the blame upon her own despair,
That she fordid herself.

ALBANY

The gods defend her! Bear him hence awhile.

EDMUND is borne off

Re-enter KING LEAR, with CORDELIA dead in his arms;
EDGAR, Captain, and others following

KING LEAR

Howl, howl, howl, howl! O, you are men of stones:
Had I your tongues and eyes, I'ld use them so
That heaven's vault should crack. She's gone for ever!
I know when one is dead, and when one lives;
She's dead as earth. Lend me a looking-glass;
If that her breath will mist or stain the stone,
Why, then she lives.

KENT

Is this the promised end

EDGAR

Or image of that horror?

ALBANY

Fall, and cease!

KING LEAR

This feather stirs; she lives! if it be so,
It is a chance which does redeem all sorrows
That ever I have felt.

KENT

[Kneeling] O my good master!

KING LEAR

Prithee, away.

EDGAR

'Tis noble Kent, your friend.

KING LEAR

A plague upon you, murderers, traitors all!
I might have saved her; now she's gone for ever!
Cordelia, Cordelia! stay a little. Ha!
What is't thou say'st? Her voice was ever soft,
Gentle, and low, an excellent thing in woman.
I kill'd the slave that was a-hanging thee.

Captain

'Tis true, my lords, he did.

KING LEAR

Did I not, fellow?
I have seen the day, with my good biting falchion
I would have made them skip: I am old now,
And these same crosses spoil me. Who are you?
Mine eyes are not o' the best: I'll tell you straight.

KENT

If fortune brag of two she loved and hated,
One of them we behold.

KING LEAR

This is a dull sight. Are you not Kent?

KENT

The same,
Your servant Kent: Where is your servant Caius?

KING LEAR

He's a good fellow, I can tell you that;
He'll strike, and quickly too: he's dead and rotten.

KENT

No, my good lord; I am the very man,--

KING LEAR

I'll see that straight.

KENT

That, from your first of difference and decay,
Have follow'd your sad steps.

KING LEAR

You are welcome hither.

KENT

Nor no man else: all's cheerless, dark, and deadly.
Your eldest daughters have fordone them selves,
And desperately are dead.

KING LEAR

Ay, so I think.

ALBANY

He knows not what he says: and vain it is
That we present us to him.

EDGAR

Very bootless.

Enter a Captain

Captain

Edmund is dead, my lord.

ALBANY

That's but a trifle here.
You lords and noble friends, know our intent.
What comfort to this great decay may come
Shall be applied: for us we will resign,
During the life of this old majesty,
To him our absolute power:

To EDGAR and KENT

you, to your rights:
With boot, and such addition as your honours
Have more than merited. All friends shall taste

The wages of their virtue, and all foes
The cup of their deservings. O, see, see!

KING LEAR

And my poor fool is hang'd! No, no, no life!
Why should a dog, a horse, a rat, have life,
And thou no breath at all? Thou'lt come no more,
Never, never, never, never, never!
Pray you, undo this button: thank you, sir.
Do you see this? Look on her, look, her lips,
Look there, look there!

Dies

EDGAR

He faints! My lord, my lord!

KENT

Break, heart; I prithee, break!

EDGAR

Look up, my lord.

KENT

Vex not his ghost: O, let him pass! he hates him much
That would upon the rack of this tough world
Stretch him out longer.

EDGAR

He is gone, indeed.

KENT

The wonder is, he hath endured so long:
He but usurp'd his life.

ALBANY

Bear them from hence. Our present business
Is general woe.

To KENT and EDGAR

Friends of my soul, you twain

Rule in this realm, and the gored state sustain.
KENT
I have a journey, sir, shortly to go;
My master calls me, I must not say no.
ALBANY
The weight of this sad time we must obey;
Speak what we feel, not what we ought to say.
The oldest hath borne most: we that are young
Shall never see so much, nor live so long.

Exeunt, with a dead march

Biography

A Short Life of Edward de Vere, 17th Earl of Oxford

by Dr. Kevin Gilvary, President
The de Vere Society

He was born on 12 April 1550 at Castle Hedingham, his family's ancestral home. His father, John de Vere, 16th Earl, was Lord Great Chamberlain and attended the coronations of both Mary and Elizabeth Tudor. His mother was Margaret Golding. Edward was 11 when, in 1561, Queen Elizabeth visited Hedingham for four days of masques, feasting and entertainments. When his father died in 1562, young Oxford left to become, like Bertram in *All's Well that Ends Well*, a ward of the Crown under the guardianship of William Cecil, the Queen's private secretary (later Lord Burghley, Lord Treasurer). His mother married Charles Tyrrell and seems to have passed out of the boy's life. His sister Mary went to live with her stepfather and the siblings were not reunited for some years.

According to a curriculum in Cecil's own hand, Edward de Vere's daily studies included dancing, French, Latin, writing and drawing, cosmography, penmanship, riding, shooting, exercise and prayer. Edward de Vere showed a prodigious talent for scholarship from his early years, and we may ascribe his lifelong love of learning to the influence of two of his early tutors. The first was Sir Thomas Smith who was, perhaps, England's most respected Greek scholar and the former Cambridge tutor of Sir William Cecil. It was, no doubt, through Cecil's

160

influence that Edward de Vere spent some time living in the household of Smith in his early years, during which time he spent about five months at Smith's alma mater, Queens' College, Cambridge. Smith was a scholar of widely varied interests – this was reflected in his 400-volume library, some of which is still extant at Cambridge. De Vere's other tutor was Laurence Nowell, who was not only an accomplished cartographer but was also England's premier scholar of Anglo-Saxon literature – it was Nowell who possessed the only known copy of *Beowulf*.

Another important influence on Edward de Vere's early studies was his maternal uncle Arthur Golding, an officer in the Court of Wards under Cecil, who is credited with the translation of Ovid's *Metamorphoses*, published in 1567, a book widely recognised as having a major influence on 'Shakespeare'.

Following on from his matriculation at Cambridge in November 1558, Edward was awarded an honorary MA by Cambridge during a Royal progress in August 1564, and another degree by Oxford University during a Royal progress in 1566. Edward de Vere then attended Gray's Inn to study law. One notable feature of the Elizabethan Inns of Court was a tradition of mounting dramatic productions and of hosting the various touring companies of players.

In 1570 he served in a military campaign in Scotland under the Earl of Sussex. By 1571, he was reported as a leading luminary of the Court and, for a time, a favourite of Queen Elizabeth. In December 1571 he married Anne Cecil, aged 15, daughter of his guardian. This was a dynastic marriage where all the advantage accrued to Cecil who, ennobled as Baron Burghley, had reduced the social gap between himself and the young Earl.

While Oxford was away on a Grand Tour of Europe, he heard that his daughter Elizabeth Vere had been born in July 1575. On his return in early 1576, he appeared to have been convinced that Elizabeth was not his child; consequently he became estranged from Anne for five years, and exiled himself from Court, taking up residence in the Savoy and concerning himself with literary and musical patronage.

Already, in 1573, *Cardanus Comfort* (the Consolations of Boethius) had been translated from Latin by Thomas Bedingfield and dedicated to Oxford; and published with a preface written by him. In 1576 an anthology, *A Paradise of Daintie Devices*, including several poems by Oxford, was published. These are juvenile works but already show affinities, in both style and thought, with those of the mature Shakespeare.

Oxford's Grand Tour had taken in Paris, Strasbourg, Venice, Genoa, Florence, Palermo and, on his way back through France, Rousillon – the setting for *Love's Labour's Lost*. Oxford spent the best part of a year travelling in Italy in 1576, and becoming involved with moneylenders. He came back to England fluent in Italian and well acquainted with the northern Italian cities, to be satirised by Gabriel Harvey as 'The Italian Earl'. On his way back his ship was attacked by pirates in the English Channel (cf. *Hamlet*). Fourteen of 'Shakespeare's' plays have Italian settings, in which he put his detailed knowledge of the country, beyond pure book knowledge, to good use.

1573 saw the birth of Henry Wriothesley, Earl of Southampton. Although history has not bequeathed to us any evidence of a direct relationship between the two men, in the relatively small world of the royal Court, they must have been acquainted with each other. The poems *Venus and Adonis* (1593) and *The Rape of Lucrece* (1594) were dedicated to Southampton. These were the first works to be published under the name 'Shakespeare' and for the next five years the records show the byline 'Shakespeare' to have been associated exclusively with these two poems. Plays under the name 'Shakespeare' did not appear in print until 1598, the year that Lord Burghley died.

In May 1577 Oxford invested in Frobisher's voyage in the ship *Edward Bonaventure*. Despite its name, the ship's voyage across the Atlantic in search of the North-West Passage lost money; consequently he was forced to sell three estates (cf. Hamlet's words 'I am but mad north-north-west' II.1.). In 1578 he invested in Frobisher's second expedition, which also lost money, forcing further sales of estates.

He was mentioned by Gabriel Harvey in an address to Queen Elizabeth in July 1578, as a prolific private poet and one 'whose countenance shakes spears'. In the same year John Lyly, Oxford's secretary, published *Euphues.The Anatomy of Wit*, followed in 1579 by *Euphues and his England*, dedicated to Oxford. These two books launched the fashion for 'Euphuism', a style characterized by high-flown language, satirized in *Love's Labour's Lost*.

In March 1581 Oxford's mistress, Anne Vavasour, who was one of Queen Elizabeth's Ladies of the Bedchamber, gave birth to a son. The lovers and their son were sent to the Tower by an infuriated Queen but swiftly released (cf. *Measure for Measure*). After his release, Oxford was wounded in a street-fight provoked by Thomas Knyvet, a kinsman of Anne Vavasour; affrays continued in the streets of London between the rival gangs of supporters for over a year (cf.*Romeo and Juliet*).

In December 1581 he resumed living with his long-suffering and devoted wife, and accepted Elizabeth

Vere as his child. Tragically, their only son died one day after his birth. Three more daughters followed, of whom Susan and Bridget survived.

In 1584, Robert Greene's *Gwydonius; the Card of Fancy* was dedicated to him, identifying him as a 'pre-eminent writer'. In 1586, when he was 36, he served on the tribunal which condemned Mary, Queen of Scots to execution.

In the same year, the Queen awarded Oxford an unconditional pension of £1,000 a year for life (about £500,000 at today's value). The motive for this uncharacteristic generosity on the part of the Queen remains a mystery – no accounting was required of Oxford. Her successor, King James I, continued to pay the pension. In reply to Sir Robert Cecil's request that Lord Sheffield's pension be increased, the King refused, saying, 'Great Oxford got no more . . .', leaving us to wonder why Great Oxford? His greatness does not seem to have resided in war or any of the known offices of State. Perhaps a clue can be found in a letter to Burghley, written in 1594, in which Edward de Vere seeks his favour in a matter involving what he describes as 'in mine office' and that this office is beholden to the Queen.

In 1589, George Puttenham published *The Arte of English Poesie* and this contains the most telling recognition of Edward de Vere's literary standing amongst his contemporaries: 'And in her Majesties time that now is are sprong up an other crew of Courtly makers Noble men and Gentlemen of her Majesties owne servantes, who have written excellently well as it would appeare if their doings could be found out and made publicke with the rest, of which number is first that noble Gentleman Edward Earle of Oxford.'

In 1588 his wife Anne, daughter of Lord Burghley, died and in extant letters written at this time, it is reported that Burghley is so incapacitated by grief over the death of his favourite daughter that he is incapable of conducting any Privy Council business.

Three years later, in 1591, Oxford married another of the Queen's Maids of Honour, Elizabeth Trentham, with whom he finally became the father of a male heir; Henry de Vere, 18th Earl of Oxford. Although there is evidence of his continued involvement in Court affairs, from the date of this marriage Edward de Vere's life at his new home at King's Place in Hackney is perhaps the most obscure of his entire life.

In 1594, his ship the *Edward Bonaventure* was wrecked in Bermuda (cf. *The Tempest*). In January 1595, Elizabeth Vere married William Stanley, 6th Earl of Derby, another literary earl who maintained his own company of players – many scholars believe that *A Midsummer Night's Dream* was written for these festivities which were attended by the whole royal Court.

On September 7 1598, Francis Meres' *Palladis Tamia* was registered for publication, naming Oxford as the 'best for comedy'. This is a vital document in Shakespearean history because it includes the first mention of 'Shakespeare' as a playwright, attributing twelve plays to him; until then Shakespeare's reputation had rested on the two narrative poems only.

Oxford suffered all his life from financial difficulties, much of which can be traced to the fact that Queen Elizabeth handed out the bulk of his estate to her favourite courtier the Earl of Leicester during Oxford's minority as a royal ward (estates which Oxford found almost impossible to reclaim), and the ruinous debt she placed upon him over his marriage to Anne Cecil. It is, however, notable that his new brother-in-law, the wealthy Staffordshire landowner and Knight of the Shire Francis Trentham, took over the management of Edward de

Vere's near-bankrupt estate from 1591 and gradually nursed it back to health so that, when Oxford died, all of his massive debts had been cleared.

On the Queen's death in 1603 Oxford wrote eloquently to Sir Robert Cecil, son and heir of Lord Burghley, of his 'great grief'. He wrote, 'In this common shipwreck, mine is above all the rest, who least regarded, though often comforted, she hath left to try my fortune among the alterations of time and chance'.

Oxford died in Hackney in 1604, cause unknown. Parish records state that he was buried in Hackney Church on July 6, but a family history by his first cousin Percival Golding, states 'Edward de Veer ... a man in mind and body absolutely accomplished with honorable endowments ... lieth buried at Westminster'. No record of such a burial can now be traced in Westminster Abbey, where there is a Vere family tomb.

The Aftermath of Oxford's life and death

During the winter season 1604-05, six of Shakespeare's plays were presented at Court by command of King James I. This has an air of commemoration. In 1609 the *Sonnets* were published in a pirated edition. The famous dedication describes the author as 'our ever-living', a phrase invariably used only of the dead.

In 1622 Henry Peacham published, in *The Compleat Gentelman*, a list of poets who made Elizabeth's reign a 'golden age'. Unaccountably, he omitted Shakespeare but placed the Earl of Oxford in first place in his list – perhaps he knew them to be the same person. This is unlike Meres who included them both – maybe one reason was because he didn't know Oxford and Shakespeare were the same person.

We do not know who instigated publication of the First Folio Edition of the Shakespeare plays in 1623, but there is no mention of any executor or relative of Shakspere of Stratford in connection with it. However, of the two brothers who financed it and to whom it was dedicated, one – Philip Earl of Montgomery – was the husband of Oxford's daughter Susan, while the other – William Earl of Pembroke – had once been a suitor for her sister Bridget. Pembroke was Lord Chamberlain, the supreme authority in the world of theatre, and thus in a position to decide which plays were to be published and which suppressed. We also know that Ben Jonson, who wrote much of the introductory material, was an intimate associate of the de Vere family after Oxford's death. The First Folio was therefore very much a family affair, but the family was not the one in Stratford-on-Avon.

An AfterVerse

For those with yet an interest
In strenuous debate
We've compiled a list of books and films
Your appetite to sate.
From this study clear your mind
Of doubt and all misgiving-
Who from us has long since gone
And who is ever-living.

Selected References & Bibliography
About the Author
Edward de Vere, 17th Earl of Oxford

Books

♦ Anderson, M. (2005). *Shakespeare by Another Name: The Life of Edward de Vere, Earl of Oxford, The Man who was Shakespeare.* New York: Gotham Books.
--A physicist by training with research interest in how evidence supports or negates a theory, Mark Anderson spent ten years investigating Edward de Vere as the author of Shake-speare's works.

♦Farina, William. (2006). *De Vere as Shakespeare: An Oxfordian Reading of the Canon.*
Jefferson, NC. McFarland & Company.

168

--Each of the plays and poems is individually assessed and explored in its own chapter, using the innumerable connections between the text itself and the life of its author, Edward de Vere.

♦ Looney, J. Thomas (2018). *Shakespeare Identified.* Cary, N.C. Veritas Publicaations.
--First published in 1920 this book began the modern Oxfordian movement. From reading it, Sigmund Freud became convinced and John Galsworthy called it "the best detective story I ever read."

♦ Ogburn, C. (1992). *The Mysterious William Shakespeare.* McLean (Va.): EPM.
--An in depth exploration and must read foundational book on the authorship question.

♦Sobran, Joseph. (1997). *Alias Shakespeare: Solving the Greatest Literary Mystery of All Time.*
New York; The Free Press, A Division of Simon & Schuster.
--A concise exploration of the puzzling questions surrounding the authorship controversy with the evidence decisively supporting the case for Edward de Vere, the 17th Earl of Oxford, as the rightful author of the Shakespeare plays and poems.

♦Whittemore, Hank. (2016), *100 Reasons Shake-speare Was the Earl of Oxford.*
Somerville MA. Forever Press.
►Also with further discussion and public comment at: *Hank Whittemore's Shakespeare Blog.*
      https://hankwhittemore.com/
--In both the book and online blog cited above, Whittemore presents a concise introduction to the

authorship question that examines 100 different aspects, from biographical and historical records, that point to Edward de Vere as the true writer of the Shake-speare plays and poems.

Websites & Videos

▶ De Vere Society. (2019). The de Vere Society – Dedicated to the proposition that the works of Shakespeare were written by Edward de Vere, 17th Earl of Oxford. [online] Deveresociety.co.uk. Available at: https://deveresociety.co.uk
--A very complete resource with substantial biographical and authorship information and links.

▶ The Oxford Fellowship (2019). Shakespeare Oxford Fellowship | Research and Discussion of the Shakespeare Authorship Question. [online] Shakespeare Oxford Fellowship. Available at: https://shakespeareoxfordfellowship.org/
--A seminal online resource especially focusing on the authorship question.

▶ Waugh, A. (2019). Alexander Waugh. [online] YouTube. Available at: https://www.youtube.com/channel/UCHN7SCKlsa9lPYJ mqqQ2uIg/featured/
OR simply search: 'Alexander Waugh'
--Alexander Waugh is a leading authorship scholar who has produced many fascinating video presentations on the authorship question. This link is to his YouTube Channel.

► Columbia Pictures & Centropolis Entertainment. (2011). *Anonymous.* Produced and directed by Roland Emmerich. [DVD]
--This mainstream film is both entertaining and enlightening. It presents a superb dramatization of the character of Edward de Vere, setting out in detail the historical and personal context which made his anonymous authorship necessary.

► Centropolis Entertainment and First Folio Pictures. *Last Will and Testament.* (2012). [DVD]
--A thoughtful and ground-breaking video documentary introduction to the Shakespeare authorship question.

Acknowledgment
Our sincere thanks to
The de Vere Society
and
The Shakespeare Oxford Fellowship
for their inspiration, help and support
in creating this series.

Attributions
--Character list from Wikipedia under
the Creative Commons License 3.0
--Play text from the Moby(tm) editions
in the public domain

Photos
Coat of Arms of Edward de Vere
Source: Wikimedia.org
Author: George Baker / Public domain

The Keep at Castle Hedingham
Source: geograph.org.uk
Author: David Phillips / CC BY-SA 2.0

The de Vere Family Coat of Arms
Source: Wikimedia
Author: Rs-nourse / CC BY-SA 3.0
(https://creativecommons.org/licenses/by-sa/3.0)

View from The Minstrels' Gallery, Hedingham Castle
Source: geograph.org.uk/p/3162585
Photo by: © PAUL FARMER - cc-by-sa/2.0

Cover/Inside: The Welbeck portrait of Edward de Vere (1575). Artist unknown. National Portrait Gallery, London.

This work has been edited and produced by

Verus Publishing
www.verusbooks.com

V | P

www.ingramcontent.com/pod-product-compliance
Lightning Source LLC
Chambersburg PA
CBHW030417100426
42812CB00028B/3001/J